The Japanese Influence on America

BOOKS ON JAPAN BY BOYE DE MENTE

The Japanese Influence on America

The Impact, Challenge & Opportunity

Boye De Mente

91-454

PASSPORT BOOKS
a division of *NTC Publishing Group*
Lincolnwood, Illinois USA

Contents

ACKNOWLEDGMENTS

I am indebted to the following "Old Japan-Hands" for reviewing the first draft of this book and making many suggestions for its improvement:

Michael Sodano
Howard van Zandt
Robert Dunham
William ("Nick") Nichoson
Steve Zimmerman
Iverson Moore
George Renwick
Paul M. Dick
Raymond Moore

Preface

Despite an intimate relationship that goes back more than one hundred years, Japan and the United States continue to misunderstand, misuse, and abuse each other. The Japanese often appear to be incapable of communicating effectively with foreign businessmen or politicans, while Americans are more likely not even to make the attempt. One result is that the "irritation threshold" that exists between our two countries is very low—and frightening.

There was some hope that the United States officially recognized Japan as having come of age as a modern nation on August 1, 1983, and would thereafter change its behavior toward the Japanese. This was the date that *Time* magazine came out with a special issue on the country entitled *Japan: A Nation in Search of Itself.*

In its prologue to the story, *Time* stated: "The name alone evokes modernity: dials, lights, and numbers. The ancient civilization, with its Shinto priests and fragile poems, is more closely associated with all that is new in our times than any place on earth. Even the New World, now graying at the temples, regularly peers east to assess the future, to note where today's advances are going for finishing touches."

Thus, in well under 100 words, *Time* acknowledged that at least the psychological leadership of the world's technological revolution had shifted from the U.S. to Japan. The magazine went on to say that Japan, "the student-nation, famous for raiding the inspirations of others," had run out of countries to copy from and now had to look to itself as a model. Japanese businessmen were referred to as "Oriental Vikings," who travel the world, studying its various languages and plundering it for every new idea they can find.

Time added that when Japan looks outward it sees that since the atom-bombing of Hiroshima in 1945 it has become a source of both wonder and fury to Western businessmen, a pressurepoint between the United States and Russia, and a global power without arms. And when it looks inward it sees a nation undergoing social and economic changes so rapidly that the next great eruption in the country might not be volcanic but human.

Time then listed some of the more conspicuous dichotomies that exist side by side in Japan—opposites that both explain and obfuscate why the Japanese are the world's new Romans: hierarchical democracy, chaotic formality, cramped infinity, ruthless ceremony, overfed wrestlers and dwarfed trees, and intense insularity combined with a deep fear of being isolated.

Japan possesses all these conflicting attributes to a certain degree, but just as the judo master turns the strength of his opponent against him, the Japanese have turned their weaknesses into advantages. Their fears motivate them to greater efforts; their rigid formalities contribute to the effectiveness of team effort; their emphasis on miniaturization has resulted in the creation of many new products.

Whatever cultural dichotomies exist within the Japanese, the sum total of their abilities, their ambitions, and their character has cast Japan in the role of an economic giant whose presence is felt around the world—and nowhere more than in the United States.

CHAPTER I

The New Romans

Japan is having a deep and pervasive influence on the United States—an influence that is far more extensive, far more fundamental, and far more important than the average American realizes. This influence is changing the fabric of American life and is therefore one of the most exciting stories of the twentieth century. I believe that it is and will continue to be overwhelmingly positive and beneficial, but many Americans do not share that opinion. In fact, many see Japan's influence as a serious threat.

So far, however, Japan is perceived as a threat only in the economic sphere. But if the country is ever viewed as anything more than a very successful economic competitor, the reaction could turn ugly.

THE GURUS OF CHANGE

Even now, the American response—in some instances, at least—is quite negative. One prominent American senator described the United States as a "benevolent chump" in its trade relations with Japan, adding that the U.S. should find some way of inflicting "economic pain on the Japanese." Another senator said: "We don't want to start a trade war, but we must convince them to play fair. We've got to make a shot across their bow to get their attention."

U.S. News & World Report quoted an American official as saying, "The next time we send a trade negotiator to Tokyo he may be sitting in the nose of a B-52!" Chimed still another political stalwart: "We need to retaliate against Japan. They deserve it!"

An editorial in *The Arizona Republic* newspaper railed against "Japan's unseeming arrogance," adding: "Americans are not so pompous that they demand incessant gestures of gratitude from friends they've helped along the way in this rough-and-tumble world. But they surely do not expect ingratitude and a slap in the face. Japan, one of the principal beneficiaries of American help, has become one of the principal ingrates of all time."

The newspaper went on to say that if Japan does not remove barriers that have made it difficult or impossible for American manufacturers to do business there, "the United States should retaliate with tariffs and quotas on Japanese products," and the U.S. "should be prepared to meet barrier-with-barrier until the Japanese get the message."

Rhetoric, yes, but such rhetoric often leads to a breakdown in communications and irrational actions that nobody wants. The threat and application of economic sanctions against Japan in the 1930s was one of the primary factors leading to war between the U.S. and Japan.

The Japanese View

In the meantime, Japanese criticism of American businessmen and government leaders is also growing in volume and vehemence. Just one example is the comments made by Hajime Karatsu, a senior adviser to Matsushita (Panasonic, National, etc.), in a recent edition of the Japanese magazine *Voice* and reported by the *Asian Wall Street Journal*. Karatsu said: "Washington today reminds me of the McCarthy era, but now it is Japan-bashing instead of red-baiting. Self-righteous witch-hunters are on the march."

Karatsu accused American businessmen of trying to blame Japan for their own failings, citing the low quality of American-made goods as the main reason why more U.S. products are not sold in Japan. "U.S. companies, it seems, don't try to reduce defects," he said. "The Japanese approach is totally different. Since the customer pays for one hundred percent of an order, any defective products that turn up later must be replaced. The customer is under no obligation to pay for a shoddy product and it is unthinkable for a Japanese manufacturer to deliberately mix defective items with good products."

Karatsu added that American businessmen must solve the quality problem before the Japanese will buy more U.S. goods and that Japanese government officials, as well as business leaders, must work harder to bring these points home to the United States.

Akio Morita, the suave and highly articulate cofounder of the Sony empire, has long had two careers—plotting strategy for the world-famous company and criticizing American businessmen for their inefficient management practices and the American government for its "irrational and unrealistic" monetary policies.

Morita has gone so far as to say that the United States is abandoning its role as an industrial power and that it is the decay of American industry that is to blame for the free-trade system's problems.

When discussing the shortcomings of American management, Morita's main points include the frequent turnover among management personnel, lack of employee security, and the failure of American companies to plan on a long-term basis.

The relationship between the United States and Japan is a very sensitive one—and has been referred to as "mutual self-deception" by columnist Joseph Kraft. The biggest threat to this relationship is that Americans will continue to underestimate the Japanese and that the Japanese will continue to take Americans for granted. It is especially dangerous for Americans to underestimate the emotional factor in Japan-U.S. relations. In Japan, human feelings come before logic, and motions often take precedence over rational thinking.

Japanese culture has been described as a "shame culture," meaning that the attitudes and behavior of the Japanese are primarily based on a deep desire to avoid shame. Once shamed, the Japanese have an equally deep compulsion to get revenge. Japan's defeat by the United States in World War II was the greatest shame that has befallen the country in its

2,000-plus year history—a shame that has only been partially expiated by the country's widely perceived economic humiliation of the Americans.

The ancient Japanese belief in their superiority is still very much alive, expressed now in cultural and economic, instead of military, terms. When the prime minister of Japan goes on national television and implores the Japanese to buy American goods and then makes a symbolic shopping trip to a department store where he buys some high-priced imports while a Caucasian blond clerk (American!) bows to him, it is proof to the Japanese that they are a superior people. After all, Japan is only about the size of the state of Montana, has almost no natural resources, and just a few decades ago was prostrate from the most destructive war in history.

It is common to hear older Japanese men say (in Japanese, of course) how glad they are that they lived to see the United States on its knees, begging Japan for help. As a lifelong foreign resident of Japan recently commented, "How many times have I heard [older Japanese men say]: 'Finally! After 40 years we've done it!'"

Of course, the Japanese publicly deny these sentiments, and much of their feeling of superiority and need for revenge are not expressed this directly, but they are there, particularly among older people, in more subtle forms.

Another factor is that the Japanese have difficulty communicating with outsiders, and both their values and aims are often misunderstood by non-Japanese.

Repaying the Debt

My purpose in focusing attention on the Japanese influence in the United States is to voice a warning and pose a challenge. The warning is that unless we rapidly learn how to do business with Japan on an equitable basis (which includes learning how to use and counter their tactics) our friendship with the Japanese could easily deteriorate into an adversary relationship. The challenge is for Americans, especially business and government leaders, to wake up to the full potential of the opportunities being presented to us by the Japanese.

In my judgment, competitive pressure from Japan is making a major contribution to the richness and ambience of American culture—in fact, I believe it is primarily responsible for the new mood of optimism and energy that is now invigorating the American economy.

Virtually all the leading "business revivalists" in the U.S. today are preaching some version of the message from Japan. These preachers, many of whom are the authors of landmark books, combine Japanese and American concepts, as well as plain common sense, in enthusiastic sermons on how to reduce costs, increase productivity, upgrade quality, be creative, take advantage of the burgeoning entrepreneurial spirit that has traditionally characterized Americans—and at the same time make American corporations more personally oriented, more human.

The exciting thing is American businessmen are *listening* to these gurus of change; they are finally *thinking*, instead of reacting from rote. Again, thanks largely to the looming shadow of Japan.

There has been a great deal of talk about the debt Japan owes the United States for the economic aid the U.S. provided in the aftermath of World War II. From my viewpoint, the lessons we have learned from Japan and the direct benefits we have derived from having to compete in our own market against Japanese goods have gone a long way toward repaying that debt.

The tidal wave of company mergers that has been rolling over the United States since the 1970s (and averaged 11 mergers a day in 1985) had its origin in Japan. In the words of *U.S. News & World Report*, the wave is "remaking" the American economy. *USN&WR* quoted economist Jerry Jasinowski of the National Association of Manufacturers as saying, "American industry is restructuring at an unprecedented pace to recapture some of its lost glory"—glory, he could have added, that has been usurped by Japan. This remaking of American business into larger, more rational economic units is making it possible for U.S. industry to be more efficient and competitive both at home and abroad—and is saving many companies from certain death.

The fact that a growing number of American corporations are now sponsoring educational programs that involve over eight million people can be traced in part to the example of Japan. Major corporations are, in effect, now operating their own universities. Xerox's 2,265-acre complex near Leesburg, Virginia, trains some 1,200 employee-students annually. AT&T's educational center near Princeton, New Jersey, has 23 classrooms, seven laboratories, an auditorium, and rooms for 300 resident students.

This is just the tip of a growing educational pyramid that is rapidly changing the face and character of education in the U.S., a development that would not have appeared almost overnight if it had not been for the extraordinary stimulation provided by the image of Japan as the new Rome.

In his book *The Share Economy*, M.I.T. economist Martin Weitzman recommends that American enterprises give up paying fixed wages to employees and adopt the Japanese system of paying workers a nominal wage, plus twice-a-year bonuses based on the individual company's revenues and profits. The traditional American reaction when growth falters and sales drop is to fire workers and cut production, increasing unemployment and contributing to the overall problems of the economy. The Japanese, on the other hand, generally do not lay off or fire workers. Income is adjusted downward so that all share in the cost of the recession.

Some commentators, including the *New York Times*, hailed Weitzman's proposal as a breakthrough in economic theory or the greatest advance in economic thinking since Keynes. Others say Weitzman is full of utopia. However, the share economy has been working in Japan for decades, and it is new only to those who have not yet discovered Japan.

Beyond Coincidence

In *Re-inventing the Corporation*, John Naisbitt, of *Megatrends* fame, recognizes that America's top 500 companies are rapidly taking on Japanese characteristics. However, Naisbitt appears to minimize the role of Japanese influence in this remarkable metamorphosis, describing it as a parallel development of what has already occurred in Japan.

But the transformations are occurring too rapidly—and the similarities are too specific and too numerous—to be coincidental. Competition in recruiting highly educated new employees, personal loyalty to the workplace, a cooperative approach to work performance, the gradual disappearance of the boss who does little but give orders, the growing importance of the human element in corporate philosophy, the increasing recognition that participation in art and other cultural endeavors is essential to the quality of life—all these changes are pure Japanese.

Among the American companies that have been conspicuously successful in recognizing and adopting key "Japanese" concepts in business management are IBM, Xerox, Motorola, and Black & Decker. Xerox, for example, instituted quality circles, significantly increased the amount of automation on their assembly lines, redesigned many of their products, added to their research and development, began planning on a long-range basis, and slashed the prices of their products to make them competitive with the Japanese.

These companies and others are, in fact, finally beginning to realize that the Japanese philosophy of putting the customer first should be the foundation for any business enterprise. By way of contrast, consider the entry of Apple Computer Inc. into Japan in 1977. Despite its amazing success in the U.S., Apple went into Japan as if the market was an extension of California. The company made no attempt to modify its computers to handle the Japanese language. Between 1977 and 1985, Apple's entire sales network was reshuffled five times, and in 1984 alone the top management in its Tokyo subsidiary was replaced twice. Finally, in 1985, the company brought in new American management with international marketing experience, began modifying its MacIntosh computer to fit the Japanese market, and initiated other steps to repair some of the damage done in the first eight years—but not soon enough to prevent several key Japanese staffers from quitting.

In her book, *Powerplay*, Mary Cunningham, a former vice president of the Bendix Corporation who became a public figure after a highly publicized affair with Bendix chairman, William Agee, argues that American corporate philosophy should be based on the "family model," in which trust, loyalty, honesty, unselfishness, and cooperation are the guiding principles. The overriding principle in the Japanese company system is that people make the enterprise: that people come first and that every company is (ideally) one big, happy family in which mutual trust and respect take precedence over all other considerations. One of the most important advantages of this more humanized, family-style approach to management is that it results in a much lower employee turnover than is typical in many American companies. A significant percentage of American companies, particularly in high-tech industries, have an employee turnover rate of up to 30 percent a year, at a tremendous cost to the companies and the national economy.

In *A Passion for Excellence*, authors Thomas J. Peters and Nancy K. Austin say that what the American labor force most needs is to be liberated from rule-ridden, top-down, and often fossilized American management. They suggest that people who are unable to conceptualize complex situations and relationships must have specific rules to guide them and to control others and that those who depend on rules generally view others with a degree of mistrust and contempt.

The authors note that America's most successful companies are therefore those that have broken the bonds of bureaucratic rules and allow their employees to be a part of the companies that employ them.

Some of the most regimented companies in the U.S. can be found in the publishing world. At one company, perhaps the most notorious for its management by rote, former employees say that the rule mentality is often carried to such an extreme that the number of windows in an office takes precedence over human factors.

One of the clearest voices in the movement to re-create the American corporation in the image of the Japanese is George Labovitz, founder and president of Organizational Dynamics Inc., a consulting firm headquartered in Burlington, Massachusetts. Labovitz says that top American management is its own worst enemy because of overcontrol. They do not allow employees to make any contribution to management, they segregate themselves from their subordinates, and they alienate the workers. The result is ill will, distrust, and lack of interest in the welfare of the company.

Some of the stories Labovitz tells about top American management illustrate such extreme stupidity that one doesn't know whether to shudder with fright or to laugh. Labovitz calls his solution to the crisis in American business "participative management"—to him, a commonsensical approach based on universal human factors. He does not mention that it is patterned directly after Japanese management.

Labovitz explains that traditional Western-style management was effective in the past, when workers were uneducated, had few, if any, rights or expectations, and were, in fact, virtually slave laborers. This system gave absolute power to management and conditioned managers to believe that their primary responsibility was to make sure that employees arrived on time and put in a full day's work and to punish them when they didn't. Management established rigid rules and commanded from the top—a system that worked very well as long as workers accepted their passive role and there was little or no outside competition. Managers trained in this system have extreme difficulty in sharing their power with workers, Labovitz adds.

Sequent Computer Systems Inc., an entrepreneurial company founded in Oregon in 1983 by Casey Powell and 16 other ex-Intel employees, is an extraordinary example of a successful attempt to create a new "company culture" based on people first and technology and products second. Virtually all the cultural concepts adopted by the company are "Japanese"—giving precedence to character, personality, and attitude in hiring new personnel, involving employees in decisions and not isolating executives behind closed doors, establishing intimate contact with employees and their families, and sponsoring meetings and workshops to perpetuate the company philosophy. *Inc.* magazine quoted Sequent marketing director, Barbara Slaughter, as saying, "How we work together, not our technology, will make or break us."

THE NEW CHALLENGE

Circumstances were to provide me with an extraordinary opportunity to pioneer in working with Japanese and American businessmen primarily to ease the cross-cultural problems they encountered, and to write the first book on the subject. Beginning in 1958, as editor of *The Importer* magazine,* published in Toyko, I interviewed hundreds of American, European, and

*During the 1950s and 1960s, *The Importer* magazine, originally called *Oriental America*, was the leading English-language trade journal covering Japan's consumer export products and played a key role in the subsequent success of many of Japan's best-known manufacturers and exporters.

Japanese businessmen about the problems they faced in doing business with each other. Since I was an outsider with some knowledge of Japan, there was a tendency for both sides to trust me and to be candid in their comments. I was thus made privy to both their problems and triumphs, and in the process I learned a great deal about the weaknesses and strengths of both sides.

In the fall of 1958, I began a series of articles in *The Importer* on the Japanese way of doing business—the practices, as well as the psychology and philosophy behind them. The articles were very popular with American and European importers, and the publisher received many requests for reprints. It quickly became obvious that I had the beginnings of what could be a successful book. I wrote several additional chapters and entitled the manuscript *Strange Bedfellows—Japanese Manners & Ethics in Business.* Later, at the suggestion of a friend at the Charles E. Tuttle Publishing Company in Tokyo, "Strange Bedfellows" was dropped from the title. Other than a study by James Abbeglen on the managerial structure and operation of a Japanese factory, *Japanese Manners & Ethics in Business (JMEB)* was the first book exclusively on the Japanese way of doing business.*

The manuscript was offered successively to McGraw-Hill and Prentice-Hall. Both turned it down, saying the market for such a book in the U.S. was too small to warrant its publication. I then offered the book to East Asia Publishing Company in Tokyo, which brought it out in December 1959.

JMEB was an immediate best-seller in the foreign community in Japan, selling as many as 500 copies a day in Tokyo alone. UPI correspondent Bob Klaverkamp (now publisher of *Asia Week*) did a story on the book that was picked up by newspapers around the world. Mail orders were phenomenal.

Hundreds of foreign companies in Japan bought dozens of copies of the book and sent them to their corporate headquarters and/or customers abroad to help substantiate some of the things they had been telling them for years—generally to no avail. The book went through four printings in less than eight months.

---

*In its latest edition, this book is now titled *Japanese Etiquette and Ethics in Business* (Passport Books, Lincolnwood, IL; 1987).

JMEB received good notices in a number of American publications, including *The Christian Science Monitor* and *Business International*. It was also picked up and used by several universities. But it was ignored by American business in general and the retail book trade. Thus the only Americans who were exposed to the book were the few thousand who were then actively involved with Japan, primarily as importers, and who bought the book in Japan or ordered it by mail.

American businessmen without experience in Japan who happened onto the book while visiting there regarded it as interesting, but something that had no special relevance to them. One particular incident stands out.

One day in 1962, I happened to walk by the bookshop in the lobby of the Imperial Hotel in Tokyo. Mrs. Kagami, the manager of the shop, was standing just outside the shop door talking to an elderly, distinguished looking man.

Mrs. Kagami glanced toward me, and said: "There he is now! Why don't you ask him?"

The man she was talking to was Eugene R. Black, then president of the World Bank, who had bought a copy of my book the day before and was discussing it with Mrs. Kagami. It turned out that Black could not accept what I had written about the Japanese way of doing business. "There is no way the Japanese could be as successful as they are if what you say about them is true!" he said to me.

Like most Americans of this era, he just could not accept the idea that any system of thought and behavior that was so different from the American approach, that was "so irrational, so illogical," could work.*

Challenge as Opportunity

The key to the continued energy, creativity, and growth of any society is some kind of threat or challenge that is met with

---

*Eighteen months after the publication of *JMEB*, I published *How To Do Business in Japan—A Guide for International Businessmen*. This was followed by *The Japanese As Consumers—Asia's First Mass Market* (with Fred Perry) and several other books on Japan. I had the market on business books on Japan entirely to myself until 1967, when Rowland Gould published *The Matsushita Phenomenon*. T.F.M. Adams and N. Kobayashi came out with *The World of Japanese Business* in 1969.

enthusiasm and confidence. During the first 160-odd years of the existence of the United States, we were blessed with immense challenges—of surviving natural hardships and disasters while settling and taming a huge continent. We were also challenged by a series of wars that, although insanely destructive, resulted in significant technical, economic, social, and political advances in a remarkably short period of time.

In the 1950s and 1960s, however, we became jaded and complacent. We became more and more dependent on the government to sustain us. Most American businessmen continued to put profit above all other considerations and thousands of them increasingly turned to Japan for cheaper products. By 1959, for example, so much of the merchandise being sold by the huge Sears Roebuck chain was made in Japan that the overall figures were kept away from the American public. This was typical of virtually all other major retail chains in the U.S. The flood of Japanese products pouring into the United States became an avalanche.

But today most of the huge volume of trade between the United States and Japan is *not* handled by American companies. It is handled by *Japanese* companies. The overwhelming majority of the imports coming *from Japan into the U.S.* are handled by *Japanese* companies with branch offices and subsidiaries in the U.S. These same branches and subsidiaries also handle *most* of the American products that are exported *to* Japan.

In 1985, for example, Mitsui *imported* close to one and a half billion dollars worth of Japanese merchandise into the U.S. and *exported* over three and a half billion dollars worth of American goods *to* Japan.

If it were not for the exporting activities of the U.S. branch offices of large Japanese trading companies, it is very probable that our trade imbalance with Japan would be far greater than it is. Japan is now doing to the U.S. what American companies have done to developing countries in Latin America and to underdeveloped nations around the world for the past century.

Of course, before we can muster the courage and energy to come out fighting, the threat or challenge has to be much more acute, much more personal. At the present time, our complacency and dependence prevent us from seeking out and facing challenges as part of our daily lives. The problem is that we do not fully understand or appreciate the human need for challenge. We have not learned that without challenge, our spirits and our intellect are stunted; our motivations are dulled.

Facing and overcoming challenges is the first fundamental step in the learning and growing process. The Japanese economic and cultural invasions of the United States may therefore rank as *one of the best things that has happened to our country since its founding.* The Japanese are forcing us to look at ourselves and our institutions in a new light. We are being forced to recognize that to remain a leader in the world's economic and political race, we must think clearly, train diligently, stay in shape—and work hard! The Japanese have done us a favor of immense proportions; not by design, but by coincidence, and we have yet to fully understand the essence or the importance of what is going on.

The Japanese have held a mirror up before us and we have been shocked at the sight, at what we have allowed ourselves to become. But we have been only partially awakened from a kind of lockstep stupor that was leading us to the tar pits—a stupor that was brought on by a failure in common sense in our government, in our corporate boardrooms, in our churches, and in our schools; and by a kind of sublime arrogance that grows out of provincial ignorance.

The Japanese, on the other hand, recognized soon after the competition became serious that they were in fact providing some of the motivation that was needed to revitalize the American people and thereby bring about a reformation of our management and industry. The Japanese have since proven their goodwill toward the U.S. by deliberately pointing out our faults and lecturing us on how to overcome them. It makes no difference that this goodwill is primarily based on their desire to continue their own economic growth and prosperity.

The Influence Epidemic

My colleague Martin Pray, who has lived in Japan off and on since 1948 as a teacher, government official, marketing consultant, and writer, has characterized Japanese influence on Americans as an "epidemic" and as "fascination fever." He says that the fever overtakes one through the eyes, ears, nose, and mouth and that the symptoms may vary from romantic delusions and paranoia to love affairs and intellectual rejection.

Pray attributes the American fascination with Japanese culture to the fact that it is totally different from our European heritage. It is this fundamental difference, he says, that attracts the interest and enthusiasm of some Americans for things Japanese, and these differences make it possible for the fascination fever to enjoy all of the trappings of a new religion. He is right, of course. But it goes far beyond this point.

There is mounting evidence that the mainstream of American culture is teetering on the edge of bankruptcy. The educational system is still off track. It continues to produce far too many high school graduates who have difficulty reading, writing, and doing arithmetic while they tend to believe the government owes them a living.

Again, primarily as a result of shocking competition from Japan (and the Soviet Union), the decline of the American school system has been slowed in some areas and actually turned around in others. In 1960, 40 percent of all high school students dropped out before graduating. Now the drop-out rate is less than 14 percent. The number of high school and college graduates who are wizards at electronics and other highly demanding disciplines is again significant and growing rapidly. Overall, however, most young Americans do not come out of the system with a good, rounded education.

One glaring example of how far the educational system has degenerated is a series of geography tests recently given to high school students. Even with maps, a significant proportion of the students could not locate some of the world's major countries.

Our political system demonstrates on a daily basis that it is incapable of meeting the economic and social challenges of the times. It is, in fact, crushing the country under the weight of mismanagement and a spiraling debt. The economic system, burdened by political irrationalities and stupidity, along with its own blind commitment to profits above all else, has finally recognized some of its faults and is struggling to overcome them, but the battle is far from won. The cultural insensitivity and blindness that is still typical of American corporations doing business abroad often results in their doing exactly the opposite of what they should be doing.

As George Renwick, president of Renwick & Associates, a Scottsdale, Arizona, consulting firm for international business, says: "The two major barriers blocking American corporate leaders in their attempts to do business overseas are arrogance and ignorance. We don't call the shots overseas like we used to. We don't speak other languages. We're not adept at dealing with people who see the world differently. We expect them to change both their way of thinking and behaving to suit us."

One of the most common examples of the weaknesses of America's multinational corporations is their failure to take advantage of the experience and insight of employees who have returned to the head offices after years of effective service abroad. These employees are often stuck in situations where their foreign experience is not used. Many of them become frustrated and quit.

Selective Imitation

I do not believe we should mindlessly ape Japanese society to the extent that we lose the wonderful qualities that have made Americans both unique and (for a long time) the envy of most of the rest of the world. What I do profoundly believe is that we should do as the Japanese do in many areas and learn from them whatever is good and beneficial to our individual lives and to the country.

A comparison of the subways in New York and Tokyo demonstrates in shocking terms the difference in Japanese and American cultural values. The subway system in Tokyo is scrupulously clean, fast, efficient, reliable, and convenient to use. Despite being extraordinarily crowded during rush hours, it is a pleasure to ride. There is virtually no vandalism and no graffiti. Crime in Tokyo's subway system is rare. In contrast, the subway system in New York was recently described by the *Washington Post* as the symbol of urban chaos and decay: "Filthy cars, urine-spattered stations, rotten tracks, stuck doors, broken lights and air-conditioning systems, rising crime rate and a rash of fires and derailments." Last year, New York transit police issued over 300,000 citations to passengers trying to evade the fare.

There are aspects of Japanese society that are irrational, inhumane, and of course damaging to the spirit and the mind.

The challenge is to select the things Japanese that have genuine merit and will in fact contribute to the quality of our lives and our constructive role in the world. And if we can have a little extra fun at the same time, so much the better!

The Japanese way of doing business cannot be imported into the U.S. intact. There are simply too many differences in the ways Japanese and Americans think and behave—ways that cannot be easily or quickly taught. But the purely human aspects of Japanese-style management can be applied anywhere. This includes common sense, treating employees as valued members of the "company family," encouraging employees to take a personal interest in the success of the company and be loyal, and providing them with the security they need to make such a commitment.

Probably the most important difference between Japanese and American businesses is that American companies are run more or less like Communist dictatorships, while Japanese companies are run more like democracies. In U.S. firms, generally speaking, plans and orders come down from the top. In Japanese companies, plans and approaches are worked out by middle management and circulated among higher executives for their approval. While Japanese companies in the U.S. are unable or unwilling to follow this system because they do not or cannot trust their American employees to behave in the expected way, they nevertheless generally attempt to apply the more universally applicable human approaches to personnel management.

Because Americans have heard that Japanese companies treat their employees differently—which is generally interpreted as meaning "better"—many are attracted by the treatment of employees in Japanese-run companies. They go to work with a different attitude. Their mood is more agreeable and cooperative. Their expectations contribute to their own fulfillment. When the Japanese companies live up to the reputation of Japanese management, the work force is happy and performs well. The atmosphere is genial; there is harmony between workers and management, and all goes well.

This book is an attempt to call attention to the areas of American life that are already becoming Japanized and to suggest other aspects of Japanese culture that I believe we should adopt as rapidly as possible.

We held the Japanese captive for nearly seven years and did our best to Americanize them. The effort was not entirely a failure, as the Japanese are the first to admit. They were delighted to accept political and social freedom and to change some of their eating habits, their style of dress, and many other relatively superficial customs. But the psychology of the Japanese remained virtually intact. The essence of their Japaneseness survived both the war and the Allied Occupation, and, as has been observed by many others, "being Japanese" is the closest thing they have to a religion.

Of course, seven years is a very short period of time—far too short to make more than a scratch on the surface of a culture as strongly entrenched and as exclusive as that of the Japanese. But even if the Occupation of Japan had lasted for twenty years or more, we would not have been much more successful in changing the Japanese. We do not have the necessary drive to deliberately reculture a large mass of people. We expect other people to adopt our ways without any special effort on our part simply because we believe our way "makes sense" and is therefore the best.

We, in fact, are far more susceptible to change than the Japanese or the people of any other well-entrenched culture. What we should do now is turn this malleability to our advantage; to utilize not only the collective wisdom of our own ethnic groups, but to import knowledge and technology from Japan without any feelings of inferiority, humiliation, or shame.

CHAPTER II

The U.S. – Japan Connection

J apanese influence in the United States—and vice versa!—has a longer history than most people realize. In 1853 the United States sent a fleet of warships to Japan to force it to end a seclusion policy that had been in effect since 1638. While this event was to have an immediate and profound effect on the subsequent history of Japan, Japan's impact on the U.S. during the remaining years of the 19th century was generally limited to architecture and the arts, and even then it was sporadic. This was to change following the Philadelphia Centennial of 1876, at which the Japanese government had several exhibition buildings and displays. Many well-to-do people with training and experience in the appreciation of arts, crafts, and architecture were overwhelmed by the beauty and serenity of Japanese designs and began to incorporate them into their homes and vacation retreats.

By the early 1900s there were few American designers who had not been influenced by Japanese concepts, and a number of those who were to become well known—particularly Frank Lloyd Wright—owe much of their later prominence to the Japanese ideas they incorporated into their work.

With the ascendancy of militarism in Japan during the 1920s and 1930s, the popular American perception of the Japanese changed for the worse. By 1940, they were regarded as the bogeymen of the East. Americans who did not know anything about the Japanese tended to look down on them as inscrutable and warlike, although quaint and exotic, and, despite their military victories over China in 1895 and Russia in 1905, as basically inferior. Few Americans believed that the Japanese were capable of creating and operating a technically advanced society.

Their small size, different skin color, coarse, straight black hair, uniformly dark eyes, unintelligible language, and such curious habits as eating raw fish and other unusual foods, were regarded in the popular American mind as self-evident proof that the Japanese were an inferior people. When World War II broke out, it was widely believed that the Japanese would not make good pilots because of their slanted eyes and generally poor eyesight. The subsequent successes of Japanese fighter and bomber pilots were attributed to fanaticism and uncivilized disregard for their own lives.

The Japanization of America began in earnest on August 28, 1945, the day the first American Occupation troops landed at Atsugi Air Base southwest of Tokyo and 13 days after Emperor Hirohito announced Japan's defeat in World War II.

After off-loading from U.S. military planes, assembling, then boarding trucks, the troops headed for Yokohama.* A few minutes after the convoy left the airport, it was met by a Japanese army vehicle loaded with young women rounded up from Tokyo's red-light districts.

An English-speaking go-between on the Japanese truck flagged down the American convoy and offered the use of the women to the Americans. The American officer in charge of the convoy refused the offer, reportedly with some vehemence, over the loud protests of many of his men.

This Japanese move, very much in character, made a profound impression on this vanguard of American troops, but it was only the barest hint of what was to come. The Japanese rationale was simple. One of the first things their troops often

---

*The first American troops did not arrive in Tokyo until September 8, 1945, over three weeks after the war ended.

did after conquering a foreign land was to go on a rape rampage. Their military propagandists had told them over and over that the American Occupation forces would do the same thing. They hoped to both blunt the edge of this primordial lust and direct it into accepted channels.

The Americans failed totally to understand the message the Japanese were sending, but they understood the medium. The warm-blooded body of a woman was something they could understand, even if it was small, plain, garishly painted, and belonged to a strange, bloodthirsty enemy popularly known as "gooks."

In the days, weeks, and months that followed this fateful meeting of vanquished foe and conquering heroes, hundreds of thousands of American men, women, and children streamed into Japan. A significant percentage of the men—married, as well as single—were soon sampling the delights of Japanese sex on a scale that has to have been witnessed to be fully appreciated. In fact, the Japanese owe much of the benevolence of the American and Allied Occupation of their country to their women. The group that tried to use sex to stop the Occupation before it got started had the right idea. They were just a little bit too early, and did not understand American psychology. As my comrade-in-writing Jack Seward would say, when the twain finally met they met and met and met.*

Well over half the Americans stationed in Japan during the Occupation years were to become enculturated with Japanitis, an affliction they carried back to the United States some year later. This infection may have begun when the overwhelming majority of the men of the Occupation forces experienced the sexual availability, prowess, and enthusiasm of a large segment of the female population of Japan. But a great number of Americans of both genders also fell in love with many of the traditional arts and crafts of Japan, eventually bringing large quantities of them back to the United States. These Americans were also impressed by some of the manners and customs of

---

*In 1952, the year the Allied Occupation of Japan officially ended, the Japanese Ministry of Health and Welfare estimated there were some 70,000 full-time prostitutes, popularly called "pan-pan girls," keeping the occupying forces busy. The MHW also estimated that the pan-pan earned around $200 million a year in hard cash. The actual number of women engaged in servicing the occupationaires was probably double the MHW's figures, and the overall income in cash and kind was probably five times the estimated figure.

the Japanese and were strongly influenced by them.

Still, the relationships that developed between most Americans and their Japanese hosts during the days of the Occupation were a combination of love, hate, bewilderment, frustration, and anger.

During the early 1950s in Tokyo, I used to despair at the robotlike behavior of the Japanese and to complain about their stereotyped attitudes toward themselves and the outside world. I felt both stifled and frustrated by their antlike response, their myopic view of the world at large, their lack of imagination, and their inability to appreciate variety and inventiveness.

I used to fantasize that one morning when the 70-some million Japanese woke up, half of them would have blond hair! The trauma would be so great, I fancied, that their *Japaneseness* would be shattered, and they would then be able to become Americanized.

As it turned out, thousands of young Japanese women began tinting their hair to varying shades of red, auburn, and brown. But only a very few—and these were mostly bar and cabaret girls—went all the way and bleached their hair blond. The reaction of the unbleached Japanese who came into contact with these courageous but misguided young women was just as traumatic as I had imagined it would be. There was, however, no measurable effect on the overall psychology of the Japanese population.

BRIEF ENCOUNTER

I first began using the phrase "the Japanization of America" and writing about this amazing phenomenon in 1958, after having served in the Occupation forces, gone to school, and worked in Tokyo over a period of 10 years. As a student of the history, culture, and customs of Japan, I had thought some years earlier that, in many ways, America was just then approaching the stage Japan reached during the latter decades of the colorful and exciting Heian Period (794–1192 A.D.), when it was synthesizing and Japanizing massive amounts of Chinese and Korean culture that were imported between the third and sixth centuries. I saw what I felt were similarities in

American attitudes toward art, aesthetics, politics, the social graces, wearing apparel, sex, the relationship between men and the cosmos, and so on.

This vision was no doubt magnified by my own fascination with and fondness for many aspects of the Japanese Way. But as the years streaked by, the vision began to turn into reality at a much faster pace than I had ever dreamed possible.

By the early 1980s, the Japanization of America had gone so far in some areas that the inevitable backlash had set in. But, in our type of open society, once such a process has started it is not likely to be slowed down or stopped, much less reversed.

The Exclusion Policy

Like many aggressive cultures, the Japanese eventually developed their own Manifest Destiny—a deeply held belief among the military and ultranationalists that Japan had a divine mission to spread its special version of harmony to the rest of the world. But it was not the empire-building impulse of the Japanese that led to our first meeting and the subsequent development of unique ties between Japan and the United States. It was our own impulse to expand our economic interests across the wide Pacific into the Empire of Japan that forged the first links between our two countries.

Americans were latecomers to Japan, however. During the Colonial period and the first 75 years of the American republic, Japan was closed to all of the outside world, except for a tightly guarded Dutch trading post permitted to operate on a tiny man-made islet called Dejima (Exit Island) in Nagasaki Harbor— which the Chinese and Koreans were also allowed to use. But only one Dutch ship a year was permitted to call at Dejima.

This exclusion policy was established by the Tokugawa Shogunate in 1638, after nearly 100 years of turmoil and change, much of it exacerbated by the presence and interference of Spanish and Portuguese missionaries and traders.

In the 1690s, Dr. Engelbrecht Kaempfer, who had been stationed at the Dutch outpost in Nagasaki for a number of years and later wrote a history of Japan, explained the policy of the Shogunate: "The voyages and travels of the natives [of Japan] into foreign countries, [and] of foreigners into Japan, were judged prejudicial to the public tranquility, forasmuch as they serve only to breed inclinations inconsistent with the nature of the country, and the genius of the Nation. In a word, whatever evil the commonwealth still laboured under, or was like to be for the future liable to, was all laid to the charge of foreign customs and Countries."

In her delightful book *The Shogun's Reluctant Ambassadors—Sea Drifters*, Katherine Plummer notes that in the late 1700s the Japanese were impressed with the fact that the American Colonies had broken away from England and become an independent nation. They were very suspicous of the motives of the English (and Russians) and apparently felt that anyone who was against the British couldn't be all bad. Thus, the first Westerner to be looked upon as a hero by the Japanese was our own George Washington.

The American Arrival

By the end of the 1700s, opposition to the Tokugawa Shogunate government was growing among Japanese scholars and several of the larger feudal fiefs, particularly those in Kyushu, who were farthest away from the Shogun's capital—and the closest to Korea and China. The scholars had learned that some 600 years earlier the first Shogun had usurped the power of the Emperor, and the Shogunate was therefore not the "legitimate" ruler of Japan. The leaders of the southern fiefs were eager to free themselves from the overseas trade and travel restrictions imposed by the Shogunate since the 1600s.

But the first Americans to approach Japan were hardly suited for the challenge of making a good impression on the suspicious Shogunate and nationalistic Samurai warriors. As Plummer notes, Captain John Kendrick of the *Lady Washington*, a trading vessel, and Captain James Douglas of the *Grace* were the first Americans of record to deliberately visit Japan. They were on their way to Osaka, but bad weather forced them to take refuge on Kushimoto-Oshima, southeast of Osaka, in May 1791. While ashore, they tried to sell some otter skins and other merchandise to the Japanese residents. Having already broken the law by landing on Japanese territory and being suspected of lying about the circumstances, Kendrick and Douglas got into more trouble by trying to peddle their otter pelts. To the Buddhist Japanese, anyone who worked with animal skins was an outcast. The two American ship captains and their men were ordered to pack up their trade samples and leave the country.

The visit of Kendrick and Douglas caused a major flap in the Shogun's Court. The Japanese remembered the problems that the Portuguese and other European nationalities had caused the country in the late 1500s and early 1600s—in addition to introducing tobacco, venereal disease, and guns—and the edicts prohibiting anyone except the Dutch (and Chinese) at Dejima from leaving or entering the country were still in force.

Shortly after the arrival of the two Americans ships, a volcano on Shimbara Peninsula erupted, destroying 27 villages and killing thousands. This disaster was immediately associated with the intrusion of the foreigners, and for decades afterward virtually all disasters in the country were blamed on the gods' being angry at the Japanese for allowing foreign ideas into the country.

During the next several years, other American ships attempted to visit Japan, but all were forced to sail away. During the Napoleonic wars, the Dutch chartered a number of American ships to carry goods to and from their trading post in Nagasaki Harbor. Among these were the *Eliza*, commanded by Captain William R. Stewart, which left New York in 1797 but was never heard from again, apparently having been lost at sea; and the *Franklin*, under the command of Captain James Devereaux from Salem, which arrived in Japan in July 1799 and stayed for four months. During this time, the crew was allowed to leave the ship for brief periods to visit brothels and go on guided tours.

As early as 1812, President James Madison was being urged to begin negotiating with Japan. An entrepreneur named David Porter wrote to Madison, "The time may be favourable and it would be a glory beyond that accomplished by any other nation, for us, a nation of only 40 years standing, to beat down their rooted prejudices, secure to ourselves a valuable trade, and make that people known to the world."

This ambitious goal was not to be easily achieved, however.

The discovery of sperm whales off of Japan's Pacific coast in 1820 resulted in large numbers of American whaling ships rushing into the waters. Ship captains were not familiar with the annual cycle of typhoons that struck the area, and shipwrecks were fairly common. Survivors who made it ashore in Japan were arrested and treated as criminals, since edicts passed in 1638 prohibited the entry of any foreigners into Japan other than at Dejima. The attitude and behavior of some of these rough, lusty castaways sometimes added to the severity of the treatment they received.

From this time on, influential Americans with interests in whaling and foreign trade began to pressure the fledgling American government to take the lead in forcing Japan to open its doors to the outside world.

The most immediate concern was to make it possible to return shipwrecked Japanese sailors to their homeland and to repatriate American seamen who had been cast on the shores of Japan and imprisoned by Shogunate authorities. The second, and no doubt overriding concern, was to obtain the right for ships to stop at Japanese ports for fuel and supplies—to be followed, of course, by the right to engage in trade with Japan.

Other nations, including England and in particular Russia, were also banging on Japan's doors in an attempt to be the first in line to establish diplomatic and trade relations with the reclusive Japanese.

In 1825, the Shogunate issued new edicts covering the appearance of foreign ships. The edicts stated that local officials should approach the ships and make inquiries. If the questions were not immediately and properly answered, all members of the crew were to be cut down with swords and the ships destroyed. If the answers were satisfactory, however, the foreigners were to be handled as peacefully as possible. But, because the religion of the intruders would be unknown, only Samurai guards were to be allowed to approach them!

President Andrew Jackson in 1835 tried to send a letter to the Emperor of Japan (nobody in the U.S. at that time knew that Japan was ruled by a Shogun), but the envoy, Edmund Roberts, died in Macau before he could get passage to Japan.

In 1837, W.C. King, an American businessman with a company in Canton, China, tried to return seven shipwrecked Japanese fishermen to Japan. When his ship approached Uraga at the entrance of Tokyo Bay, it was fired on by shore batteries of cannon, driving him off.

King then sailed to Kagoshima at the southern tip of Kyushu, hoping to have better luck there. At first, he was greeted without any hostile action. A local official boarded his vessel, provided him with a pilot, and told him a senior government official would arrive the following day to discuss the return of the fishermen.

Later that evening, a friendly boatman warned King that he and his men were to be arrested and his ship confiscated. King quickly made preparations to sail out of the harbor. His ship immediately came under fire but was able to escape unharmed. He returned to China with the Japanese fishermen still aboard his vessel.

When news of this incident reached the U.S., there was a great deal of indignation. The repercussions in Japan were even stronger. Several Japanese who criticized the actions of the Shogunate were imprisoned, ostracized, or forced to commit suicide.

Eight years later (1845), another American vessel, the *Manhattan*, under the command of Captain Mercator Cooper, appeared off the coast of Uraga (near present-day Tokyo) with a number of Japanese fishermen who had been picked up while adrift in the Pacific. This time, the fishermen were allowed to disembark and return to their homes because they had not touched foreign soil.

In 1846, the U.S. sent Commodore James Biddle and two ships to Japan with a letter from President Polk addressed to the Emperor, requesting that diplomatic and trade relations be established. After several very touchy days, during which Biddle was knocked down by a Samurai, the Shogunate authorities refused to accept the letter and ordered Biddle to leave. This caused further indignation in the U.S.

In 1848, a group of 15 men deserted an American ship in Hokkaido, Japan's northernmost main island, apparently because of rough treatment aboard the vessel, and were immediately arrested and imprisoned by the authorities. They were a rough bunch. Some of them were put into stocks. Three who escaped were quickly captured and put into small cages—the same type of cages used to house and transport dangerous Japanese convicts.

Another incident (recounted by Katherine Plummer) involved a young American adventurer, Ranald McDonald, who was part Chinook Indian and had met some young Japanese shipwreck survivors in Vancouver. McDonald became intrigued with the idea of going to Japan, studying the Japanese, and teaching them about the West.

He obtained a job on a whaler headed for the waters off Japan. Once there, he talked the captain into putting him ashore in a rowboat. He landed on a small deserted island off the coast of Hokkaido. Found some time later by Ainu fishermen from Hokkaido (the aboriginal natives of the Japanese islands), he was turned over to Shogunate authorities, who immediately put him in prison.

McDonald was young, clean-cut, serious, and well educated, and he carried a load of books. The Japanese authorities liked him and sent him to distant Nagasaki in the far south of the country, Japan's only window to the outside world.

In Nagasaki, McDonald was kept confined but was under the direct jurisdiction of the governor of the city, who told him he would be treated well as long as he behaved himself. He was allowed to teach English to a select group of government interpreters, one of whom, Enosuke Moriyama, was later to play a prominent role in the first trade and diplomatic negotiations between Japan and the United States.

In 1849, Commander Glynn of the USS Preble sailed into Nagasaki Harbor with guns bristling. He gave the local authorities an ultimatum, saying they had three days to deliver all American castaways to his ship. Just before the expiration of the deadline, local Shogunate authorities delivered the young Ranald McDonald and the 13 survivors from the group that had deserted in Hokkaido the year before, for repatriation to the U.S.

In the meantime, ferment in Japan was reaching a boiling point. Talk of a revolution was underway. Enemies of the Shogunate were determined to restore the Emperor to power. They regarded the Shogunate's inability to cope with the encroaching foreign powers as proof that it was no longer capable of ruling the country.

A squadron of American ships under Commodore John H. Aulick set sail for Japan in June 1851, intending to stop over in Hong Kong and pick up 17 Japanese castaways who had been dropped off there over the years. Aulick was suddenly recalled to Washington, D.C., and Admiral Matthew C. Perry was appointed to replace him.

It was early 1853 before Perry arrived in Shanghai to take over Aulick's squadron of twelve black warships, and it was

July 8, 1853, when the squadron arrived in Tokyo Bay. The Japanese had never seen steam-powered warships before. The sight of Perry's black fleet belching smoke and steaming up the Bay caused an uproar in the Shogunate capital of Edo (Tokyo).

After some very tense formalities, the Shogunate authorities agreed to meet Perry at Kurihama, south of Tokyo. There he delivered his presidential letter addressed to the Emperor and told the Japanese he would be back the following year for their answer.

The presidential letter that Perry presented to the Shogunate officials stated that the U.S. wanted a fueling station in Japan for merchant ships, a trade agreement, and diplomatic relations. The letter implied that if Japan did not agree to these concessions voluntarily, the United States would force them onto Japan!

The Emperor in Kyoto, who was only the spiritual head of Japan, and his advisors opposed the signing of the agreement with the U.S. But, without a navy, the Shogunate also knew it could not prevent the United States or any of the other foreign naval powers from imposing their will on Japan.

The Open Door

Realizing it was no longer able to maintain the exclusion policy that had prevailed for over 200 years, the Shogunate finally agreed to establish limited relations with the U.S. upon Perry's return—with the idea that thereafter it would use delaying tactics to stave off any further involvement with outsiders for as long as possible (a tactic the Japanese still use with considerable skill).

Perry and his awe-inspiring ships returned in March 1854. He had his first meeting with Shogunate negotiators on March 8 at Kanagawa (now Yokohama). Following several days of negotiating, the *Treaty of Kanagawa* was signed.

The treaty opened two Japanese ports to American ships and traders. The first one, a small fishing village called Shimoda, was isolated near the end of Izu Peninsula. The second one was to be designated later. The treaty also called for the stationing of an American Consul in Japan (the later-to-be-famous Townsend Harris, who arrived in Shimoda in August 1855).

Thus it was that the United States played the leading role in forcing Japan, after 215 years of self-imposed isolation, to open its doors to the outside world (just beating out Russia, whose envoy also arrived in Nagasaki in 1853 with similar demands), beginning a relationship that was to be remarkable in many ways and would eventually see the roles of the two countries virtually reversed.

Following the signing of the Treaty of Kanagawa, nationalists immediately rallied around the Emperor and speeded up their plans to overthrow the Shogunate. Their slogan was *Sonno Joi!* (Revere the Emperor! Drive out the Barbarians!).

Led by young firebrands from clans in southwestern Japan, the nationalist forces defeated the inexperienced armies of the Shogun. These new leaders, like so many warriors before them, pledged allegiance to the emperor in Kyoto, then a young boy named Mutsuhito. They had the boy emperor and his court moved into the Shogun's castle in Edo. Later, the name of the city was changed to Tokyo (Eastern Capital).

Although Mutsuhito grew up to be an intelligent and hardworking monarch (whose official name was to be Emperor Meiji), the young rebels who had toppled the Shogunate continued to control the new parliamentary type of government that was formed, with the Emperor little more than an advisor.

A CENTURY OF WAR AND EXPANSION

It was not until the opening of several ports to trade in 1859 that substantial numbers of Americans began arriving in Japan. One of the first was Henry Holmes, a ship captain who had made several successful trips to the Orient prior to the opening of Japan and was the first one to register as a foreign merchant, even before the Kanagawa treaty came into force in February 1859. Holmes later noted in his journal: "They (the Japanese) will surprise the world!"

There could hardly have been two more dissimilar peoples than the Japanese and Americans. The Japanese were small of stature, with very little facial and body hair. They had a highly sophisticated, meticulously structured political system, a minutely detailed social etiquette, a stern dress code, and *they took hot baths every day!*

The first Americans, as well as virtually all the Europeans, who had visited Japan in the early 1800s were seaman—in many cases, castaways from whaling boats that were wrecked in the annual typhoons that swirl around and over the islands. Generally huge by Japanese standards, often with copious body-hair and full, bushy beards, these men dressed in rough clothing (sometimes made of leather, which made them untouchable), had absolutely barbaric manners, as far as the Japanese were concerned, and seldom bathed.

The Americans who followed the seamen were several cuts above this level, but were still barbaric-looking and -acting aliens to the previously isolated and insular Japanese. The closest analogy the Japanese had to Westerners were mythological *Tengu*—huge, hairy, bearded, long-nosed, devil-like creatures who came down out of the mountains to rape women and terrorize children.

Industrialization and Colonization

Having committed itself to entering the world stage, Japan's new government under Emperor Meiji and his young ex-Samurai advisors undertook the challenge with a degree of energy and ambition that was a precursor of what was to come. The newly established government began by engaging foreign experts— primarily from England, Germany, and the United States—to come in and help them remake the economy of the country. For the next two decades, these thousands of foreign specialists were instrumental in transforming Japan from an agricultural and cottage-industry society into a modern-day, world-class industrial power.

Aping the colonial powers of Europe that were anxious to carve up and control the rest of Asia, Japan attacked China in 1894, winning a number of territorial concessions. This was followed by war with Russia in 1904 (which ended in 1905, with the United States acting as mediator), and the awarding of additional territorial concessions to Japan.

In 1910, Japan annexed Korea. Four years later, Japan entered World War I on the side of the Allies, ending up with several Pacific island groups when the war ended. Japan later announced its Greater East Asia Co-Prosperity Sphere, which the rest of the world understood as a signal that Japan intended to dominate all of Asia. Under pressure from the United States, Japan signed a Five-Power Naval Disarmament Treaty in 1922, limiting its naval power in relation to that of the U.S., England, and other leading European nations.

In 1932, fighting broke out between Japanese and Chinese troops in Manchuria. The following year, Japan in effect made the huge area a part of the growing Japanese empire. The Japanese government withdrew from the League of Nations in 1933 and in 1934 canceled the naval limitations agreement it had signed with the U.S.

Japan began full-scale war against China in July 1937 and over the next four years conquered virtually all of southeast Asia. The U.S. began applying various economic sanctions against Japan, prohibiting the export of scrap iron and steel, etc., in an attempt to stop the spread of war. In a preemptive strike to prevent the U.S. from interfering with its military conquests in Asia and the Pacific, the Japanese bombed the American naval base at Pearl Harbor in the Hawaiian Islands on the morning of December 7, 1941.

The war between Japan and the United States was a great surprise and disappointment to many Japanese and Americans. Despite the dissimilarities, there had always been an exceptional amount of goodwill and admiration between the two nations. There was a sizable population of Japanese in this country. Thousands of Japanese had gone to school in the U.S. and had close friends here. Americans admired the discipline, the sophisticated manners, the graciousness, and hospitality of the ordinary Japanese. The Japanese admired the freedom, the inventiveness, the industriousness, and the friendliness of Americans.

It should not have been a surprise when all of this goodwill—and more—resurfaced at the end of the war, and most Japanese eagerly offered themselves up to being made over as Americans. As mentioned earlier, however, we Americans were just as susceptible to change as the Japanese were, and the stage was set for the Japanization of America by our Occupation of Japan from 1945 to 1952.

American Attitudes

As the Japanese military forces overextended themselves and began to lose to American and Allied forces—which gradually became overwhelmingly superior in numbers and firepower—the American superiority complex soared to new heights. With the arrival of American Occupation troops in Japan in 1945, there was nothing to change the common American opinion that the Japanese were inferior. The country was physically devastated by war. The people were hungry, exhausted, demoralized, and frightened—hardly in shape, physically or spiritually, to impress anyone.

Furthermore, Japan's traditional etiquette, made up of an extreme form of ceremonial politeness, was regarded by many Americans, men in particular, as a negative factor—as obsequious, insincere, feminine, and often just plain stupid. This category of Americans included those who referred to the Japanese as "gooks"—a term that apparently comes from the word *Hangook*—"Great Nation"—which is what the Koreans call their country.

There could hardly have been a more disrespectful term than *gook*. It went beyond denigrating the Japanese. It dehumanized them—and it was all the justification "gook users" needed to abuse and further insult the Japanese.

As the years of the Occupation passed, the category of American GI's who were uneducated, insensitive, and arrogant and referred to the Japanese as gooks was gradually joined by a comparable breed of American businessmen, whose superiority complex knew no bounds. These men treated the Japanese with varying degrees of arrogance and contempt. The worst ones constantly railed at their Japanese suppliers and behind their backs described them as "jerks," "imbeciles," and worse.

Even some of the more understanding Americans tended to regard the Japanese with a kind of condescending tolerance that adults often display toward children. These were generally the ones who developed a genuine appreciation for many aspects of Japanese life and art—but as is so often the case, they were likely to admire the arts and crafts more than they did the people who created them.

Then there were the large number of Americans of the Occupation whose primary attraction to Japan was sexual. They had easy access to the hundreds of thousands of women in the legal red-light districts, "GI bars," and massage parlors who made the Japan of that era a playboy's paradise. Some of the relationships that developed between these men and their

Japanese girlfriends led to marriage. Unfortunately many of these unions were based on convenience and physical satisfaction and often had tragic consequences.

Some of the Americans in this category were unable to reconcile their ambivalent feelings toward the Japanese. They developed an intense love/hate relationship that in many cases virtually ruined their lives and the lives of the Japanese with whom they had developed intimate bonds. These were often people with extremely low self-esteem, who first of all disliked themselves and used the Japanese as scapegoats to assuage their own feelings of inadequacy. They often stayed in Japan for year after year, despite the agony they inflicted on themselves and others, in part because of the sensual aura cast by Japanese culture.

Japan's Postwar Success

As the Japanese penchant for hard work, coupled with their extraordinary drive to excel, began to pay off in a rapidly rising standard of living, a curious attitude developed among large numbers of Americans who worked in and with Japan. They couldn't believe that the Japanese were capable of achieving such success. They were mostly the people who still believed in their own innate superiority over the Japanese—throwbacks to the World War II period, when "Japs" were funny little people who wore glasses and copied everything.

When the Japanese continued to reach higher and higher plateaus of success, most of these Americans began to rationalize the achievements of the Japanese by attributing them to the openness of the American market and the unfair tactics of Japan's export industry and government.

The provincial outlook and superiority complex of many American businessmen allowed them to conclude that because the Japanese way of doing business was incompatible with "modern, sophisticated" business practices it would have to be totally discarded and replaced by the American system.

In the early 1950s, a few Japanese businessmen, unsure of themselves and intimidated by the aggressive approach of Americans, attempted to convert their companies to the American style of management. Most of the attempts ended in failure. Other Japanese companies that had been flirting with American management knew a bad thing when they saw it and quickly went back to traditional Japanese ways of managing their enterprises—keeping only the American ideas that could be adapted to their way of doing things.

Following this period, there was a resurgence of faith in the Japanese Way, particularly among such outstanding business leaders as Konosuke Matsushita, founder of the fabulously successful Matsushita Electric Industrial Company (National, Panasonic, etc.); Sazo Idemitsu (Idemitsu Oil); Soichiro Honda, founder of Honda Motor Company, and Taizo Ishizaka, president of Toshiba and the Keidanren (Federation of Economic Organizations), who was conspicuously pro-American and advisor to many foreign companies.

Matsushita, who was to become the great guru of Japanese-style management, advocated the practice of meditation and contact with "cosmic consciousness" as part of the training for effective management. This caused typical American businessmen to snicker in their martinis and reinforced their belief that Japanese management was a feudalistic anachronism that had no place in the modern world.

One American company after another set up branches in Japan, brought in their way of doing business, and got set to make a killing. Some of these companies struggled for years and went through millions of dollars before giving up and pulling out. The American businessmen who succeeded in Japan were the ones who finally acknowledged that the American way did not work there and combined the American and Japanese management principles.

During the 1960s and early 1970s, Japan's economic juggernaut gained weight and momentum. The Japanese business system was honed to a fine edge, and they became the new Romans, spreading the Greater Japan Economic Prosperity Sphere around the globe. In the meantime, American business, often adversely influenced by powerful labor unions, became flabby, complacent, weak willed, and confused. It lost the spirit, the drive, and the inventiveness that in earlier decades had made America the envy of the world.

Then came the oil and dollar shocks. Japan emerged from these traumatic experiences stronger still, while the U.S. was shocked and began reeling like an out-of-condition boxer. This set the stage for the appearance of a spate of books advocating that American managers begin learning from the Japanese. In the mid-1970s, several American scholars discovered Japanese management and began suggesting that there just might be something American businessmen could learn from Japan.

Then, in one of the great flip-flops of history, American businessmen went from deriding Japanese management to trying to figure out ways of adapting it to their own business.

This was also the signal for a frenzy of magazine articles about Japan, its culture, and its unique management system. One writer after another gave his blessing to the idea that it was all right for American businessmen to understudy the Japanese—that the crises in American management was serious enough that some un-American behavior was indeed permissible.

Finally, after nearly twenty years, the American educational and publishing establishments began picking up on the Japan story.

CHAPTER III

"Big Tokyo" USA

W e have heard a lot about rich Japanese companies and individuals buying big chunks of American real estate, and they have. In addition to the initiative of Japanese investors in the U.S., the economic development departments of many American states have been actively seeking Japanese industrial investments in their areas since the early 1960s.

Japanese investment in American real estate really took off in 1980, when the Japanese government eased its restrictions on the movement of capital abroad. By 1984, holdings had reached $663 million and were expected to jump to around $1.3 billion by the end of 1985. While moving cautiously, nearly all the Japanese investors in U.S. real estate say they are just getting started. They are able to undercut American investors because they are willing to accept lower returns on their investments. Once the Japanese buy a piece of property, they almost never sell it.

There are indications that the huge Japanese pension funds will become increasingly active in the U.S., which could make the present buying binge pale by comparison. Kevin F. Haggarty, executive vice president of Cushman & Wakefield, predicts that foreign investment in American real estate will be dominated by the Japanese for the rest of the twentieth century.

Just as significant has been the "recycling" of Japan's huge trade surplus with the U.S. into the American financial market.

It is estimated that Japanese investors are buying U.S. Treasury notes at the rate of $1 billion a month—notes that pay them approximately double the amount of interest they could earn by similar investments in Japan. Japanese banks have passed American banks in making syndicated international loans.

In February 1985, Japan's huge Mitsui Bank estimated that Japan had become the world's largest creditor nation, outstripping Britain and the United States. The main cause of Japan's surging to the forefront was an increase in investments in foreign bonds by Japanese companies.

Cash-rich Japanese banks themselves are in the forefront of the movement of Japanese companies into the United States. At this writing, 24 Japanese commercial banks have branches or agencies in the U.S., and they are becoming more and more active in merger and acquisition operations. Japanese banks already own three of the ten largest banks in California. Mitsubishi Bank, which bought the Bank of California in June 1984 for $230 million, has set up special units in California and New York to advise Japanese companies on managing their investments in the U.S. and establishing tax shelters in the Bahamas. Japanese banks in the U.S. are also emphasizing risk-free fee-earning activities, such as letters of credit for tax-exempt municipal bonds.

An additional example of the extent of Japanese penetration into American business is the printing of U.S. passports—often the very symbol of the United States. Uno Seisakusho Company, the maker of a highly automated passport manufacturing system, beat out both American and European bidders to supply the U.S. Government Printing Office with Japanese-made machines to print passports. Uno also won a Printing Office contract to supply a postcard cut-and-pack system.

Japanese investment in the United States is, of course, primarily aimed at avoiding American trade barriers and providing Japanese manufacturers with specific marketing advantages, such as lower transportation costs, better follow-up service, and faster market research—all resulting in their obtaining a larger share of the American market that much faster.

ON THE MAINLAND

It is important to keep in mind, however, that the Japanese expansion into the U.S. real estate and banking industries (among others) is not entirely new. Indeed, Japanese-Americans have been landowners and investors since their arrival here many decades ago. And the combined influence on American life of well-established and growing Japanese-American communities *and* the current high and rapidly expanding level of Japanese exports of people, products, money, and marketing principles is now—and will continue to be—profound.

It used to be that the only conspicuous areas of Japanese influence in the United States were the "Little Tokyo" sections of downtown Los Angeles and San Francisco, where there were concentrations of Japanese-style restaurants and shops run primarily by Americans of Japanese ancestry. Now there are also very large and very conspicuous communities of Japanese nationals in many areas of the United States.

Besides the proliferation of even more Japanese restaurants and shops in the U.S., there are Japanese-language newspapers and Japanese television programs. Thousands of people in the enclaves to which these media are addressed do not speak English and are under very little pressure to learn the language. They get by with Japanese.

There are some 4,000 Japanese-owned and affiliated companies in the U.S. Altogether, the jobs of some one million Americans are based on the activities of these companies. The economic viability of dozens of American cities is dependent on Japan to significant degrees.

New York and Chicago

New York's Japanese community, made up of businessmen, their families, students, artists, and various other categories of people, is approximately 100,000 strong. There are over 1,500 Japanese artists in the New York City area alone. Most of the businessmen and their families are stationed in New York for three to five years and then replaced by newcomers. This continuing cycle of new arrivals provides the community with a sense of freshness and dynamism.

In addition to these semipermanent Japanese residents in New York, an estimated 500,000 Japanese tourists visit the city every year. New York has its own *Japanese Yellow Pages (JYP)*, a bilingual directory of Japanese businesses and other useful services, published annually by Japan Hour Association Inc.

JYP also covers restaurants, tourist services, and related facilities in Washington, D.C., Boston, and the New England area.

This Japanizing process goes well beyond the Japanese community itself. Some dozen public high schools in New York offer Japanese studies programs that cover the language, the culture, and current events in Japan. One of the most comprehensive and successful of these programs is the one conducted by social studies teacher Mike Lustig at John Dewey High School in Bensonhurst. Begun in 1973, Lustig's classes are lively and unorthodox. He has his students role-play, takes them on field trips, invites Japanese experts in, and uses video films of live scenes taped in Japan to help his students get a better feel for the language and culture.

One of the most extraordinary events to take place in New York in recent years was a tournament staged by 38 of Japan's huge sumo wrestlers at Madison Square Garden. Sumo is an ancient, ritualistic sport that evolved from the very heart of Japanese culture and is as traditionally Japanese as anything can be. Commenting on why New Yorkers would be attracted by such a typically Japanese experience, John Wheeler, vice president of the Japan Society in New York and an expert on the sport, told *The Asian Wall Street Journal:* "Foreigners are captivated by the color of the sport. In all of this stately pageant, this panoply of sight and sound, these two huge guys explode in a burst of action that's over very quickly. It's uniquely Japanese."

In 1985, Japanese businessmen Eizo Kawamoto, president of U.S.-Nippon Communications Network, launched a three-hour weekly television show primarily designed to appeal to New York's Japanese community and to serve as a communications channel between the community and the New York business world. One segment of the show, called "Business Nippon," covered the activities of some of the more successful American companies in Japan. This segment became an instant hit with New York businessmen interested in learning more about the Japanese market and how to do business in Japan.

The state of Illinois is a major agriculture exporter to Japan. Chicago, as the principal trading center in the Midwest, is regional headquarters for such Japanese trading giants as Mitsubishi, Mitsui, Marubeni, Sumitomo, Kanematsu-Gosho, Toyomenka, and Nichimen. Japanese banks in the city include the Bank of

Tokyo, Dai-ichi Kangyo, Sumitomo, Sanwa, Fuji, Hokkaido-Takushoku, Saitama, Taiyo Kobe, Tokai, and Kyowa.

Before World War II, the Japanese community in Chicago consisted of about 300 Japanese-Americans and a few Japanese nationals working for trading and shipping companies. Partly because the group was small, the Japanese-Americans were not interned during the war years. When the War-Relocation Authority began releasing Japanese-Americans from internment camps after 1942, some 30,000 of them moved to Chicago, where many stayed after the war ended.

In 1950, the Japanese-American population in Chicago was about 11,000. By 1980 it was over 16,000. Just as on the West Coast, nearly half of all Japanese-American marriages in Chicago are with non-Japanese partners. There is very little interaction between the Japanese-American residents of Chicago and the fairly large community of Japanese nationals, however. The Japanese-Americans say the latter are aloof and condescending.

Japan expert Iverson Moore, who now lives in Chicago, notes that the evidence of Japanese influence in the city includes restaurants (the famous Hatsuhana has a branch there), groceries, travel agencies, numerous other small businesses, Japanese bookstores, libraries, Japanese language courses at several universities and colleges, weekly television programming, and a Japanese-language newspaper, the *Chicago Shinpo*.

Several local film societies devote interest to Japanese films, with the result that films can be seen almost weekly (listed in a free weekly newspaper called the *Reader*). There is also an Asian-American theater group, Minna-Sama no Gekijo, founded by Japanese-American actress Shuko Akune, which gives occasional performances.

Japanese theatrical techniques, taught by visiting Japanese groups and Professor Shozo Sato, a Japanese playwright-teacher at the University of Illinois, have had a strong influence on Chicago's off-Loop troupes. Professor Sato is widely regarded as Japan's leading cultural ambassador to the United States. One American actor described these classes as "the greatest spiritual experience of our lives."

The Buddhist Education Center at 4645 North Racine offers courses in the Japanese language, as well as sumi-e (woodblock printing), calligraphy, bonsai, tea ceremony, Buddhist philosophy, Sanskrit, and other subjects. The Chicago Kimono School is said to be the only such school in the U.S., and over half of its students are non-Japanese. The congregation of the Midwest Buddhist Temple includes a growing number of non-Japanese Americans, and worship services are now held in both English and Japanese. The temple also conducts Zen meditation, operates a Japanese-language school, and sponsors an annual Ginza Holiday in August.

Toguri's Mercantile Company, operated by Mrs. Toguri d'Aquino (the famous "Tokyo Rose" of World War II), is the city's leading supplier of the material things one needs for living Japanese style. Aiko's Art Supply offers a vast array of supplies and equipment for Oriental art and calligraphy and includes a gallery specializing in modern Japanese printmakers.

One of the most interesting and important areas of Japanese influence in Chicago is a Japanese-language course and mathematical study program at the Murray Language Academy (the first public elementary school in the U.S. to offer daily instruction in Japanese), conducted by Japanese-language teacher Mrs. Itsuko Mizuno.

Mrs. Mizuno, who was born and raised in Japan, was appalled at the low quality of math textbooks her own children brought home from school and the poor mathematical ability of the students graduating from the school. After she began teaching at Murray in the 1970s, she introduced the abacus into her classroom and began drilling the students on basic mathematical concepts, having them shout out the answers as they clacked away on their abacuses. The results were amazing. "The abacus trains children in self-reliance, discipline, and a thorough under-standing of the decimal system," Mrs. Mizuno said.

In her Japanese-language course, which students begin in kindergarten and continue daily all the way through the eighth grade, Mrs. Mizuno explains to her students that there are reasons other than business for studying Japanese, such as broadening one's view of the world by learning something about the values and culture of a society that is profoundly different from the American.

The West Coast

Some parts of Seattle look like suburbs of Tokyo or some other

Japanese city. The first Japanese arrived in Seattle in 1878. There are now some 23,000 Japanese-Americans and over 5,000 Japanese nationals living in the city. Some 100 Japanese firms have branch offices and/or factories in the Seattle area. Leaders of the Japanese business community in Seattle and corporate home offices in Japan are becoming more and more active in promoting cultural and educational programs aimed at widening understanding and interchanges between the city and Japan.

Seattle and Kobe have been Sister Cities since 1959. Seattle sent the first postwar trade mission to Japan.

A Japanese company in Everett, Washington, Kohkoku USA, a manufacturer of vinyl sheeting, provides material for some 40 percent of all the waterbeds sold in the U.S. The company operates nonstop, 24 hours a day, and when it can't keep up with demand it imports vinyl sheeting from its parent company in Japan. Kohkoku is a popular company in Everett. American business in the Northwest often points to it as an outstanding example of how a Japanese company with superior technology, marketing, and management expertise is a successful, dynamic part of the community.

Japan's largest shipping companies (Nippon Yusen Kaisha, Mitsui, OSK, Yamashita-Shinnihon, and Kawasaki Kisen) were the first group of foreign shipping firms to establish a major base of operations in Seattle and make the city the world's seventh largest container port. A major share of the trade between Japan and Alaska passes through the Seattle, Tacoma, and other Puget Sound ports.

The first Japanese ship to enter the transpacific "Silk Lane" trade was the *Miike Maru*, owned by Nippon Yusen Kaisha. It arrived in Seattle on August 31, 1896. Today the Japan Six Lines lease all of the 93-acre Terminal 37 from the Port of Seattle and use it exclusively for their containership services.

One of the oldest Japanese tenants in Seattle is Mitsui & Co. Its office was opened there in 1916 by a young man named Reisuke Ishida, who later was to become the director-general of Japanese National Railways.

Other leading Japanese companies in the Seattle area include C. Itoh, Asahipen (Japan's largest producer of do-it-yourself paint products), and Nippon Suisan (Nissui). Seattle, the closest U.S. port to Japan, is 300 miles nearer than San

Francisco/Oakland and 600 miles closer than Los Angeles/San Pedro and likes to refer to itself as "The Boston Harbor of the New World of the Pacific Rim."

Few Americans would ever suspect that the new Boeing 767 plane made by the Boeing Company (the world's largest commercial aircraft manufacturer) is an American-Japanese hybrid. A substantial part of the plane, including components for the body section, are produced in Japan, shipped to Boeing in Seattle, and there fitted into the new planes. Says the president of Boeing, "Everything is delivered on time and fits perfectly."

Local authorities predict that tourism will be the No.1 industry in the state of Washington by the early 1990s and that Japanese tourists will make up a significant percentage of the visitors.

San Francisco has had direct links with Japan since 1867, when the Pacific Mail Steamship Company (one of the predecessors of the American President Lines) inaugurated regular service to Japan with a fleet of five wooden, paddle-wheel, steam-powered ships designed to carry flour, silver, and gold to the Orient and bring back silk, tea, and rice.

The city now has a large and steadily growing community of Japanese-Americans, as well as Japanese nationals, including students and employees of Japanese companies. The Japan Center at 1581 Webster Street, with its dozen of shops and restaurants, is a major attraction.

The several hundred companies in San Francisco include banks, trading companies, securities firms, advertising agencies, printing companies, real estate and development companies, construction firms, marketing and research firms, shipping companies, and manufacturers. Their employees and employee families, along with Japanese students, artists, and sundry other people, make up a sizable community of Japanese nationals in the city.

In 1984, the Mitsui Group of 28 companies in San Francisco set up a Mitsui Public Relations Committee to stage a series of public activities called "Close-Up of Japan in San Francisco." The opening of the activities was marked by a reception at the St. Francis Hotel, which was attended by over 500 political, business, and cultural leaders and presided over by Mayor Dianne Feinstein. The activities included a two-month-long fashion show, handicraft exhibitions, lectures, flower arranging, and even the showing of Japanese television commercials, which were one of the hits of the program.

As a major gateway for tourists, as well as businessmen, from Japan, San Francisco annually plays host to several hundred thousand Japanese.

One of the largest concentrations of Japanese on the West Coast is in the Torrance and Gardena areas of Greater Los Angeles. When you drive around in these industrial areas, practically every other company sign you see is Japanese. In Torrance, for example, 182nd Street might very well be called *Nippon-dori* (Japan Street).

There is a constant stream of Japanese businessmen passing through the city's hotels, and each year hundreds of thousands of Japanese tourists flock to Los Angeles to visit Disneyland, Hollywood, and other attractions. A very conspicuous indication of the importance and influence of these Japanese guests throughout the Greater Los Angeles area is the number of signs in Japanese in hotels, restaurants, and other places of business.

Many of the thousands of groups of Japanese that troop into Los Angeles annually are met at the airport by local representatives of Japanese travel agents who stay with them during their entire visit, acting as guides and interpreters, and making sure that their experience is sufficiently Japanized to keep them content. For the majority of these people, Los Angeles has become an extension of Japan.

The influence of Japanese businessmen and tourists on Los Angeles is spilling over into the Japanese-American, as well as the non-Japanese, community. Japanese-language television shows and newscasts are aired daily. The number of non-Japanese patronizing Japanese restaurants, food stores, and other Japanese businesses in the area is growing rapidly.

A very popular annual event in Los Angeles is "Nisei Week," held in mid-August. *Nisei* means "second generation" and refers to Japanese-Americans who were the first generation of Japanese to be born in the U.S. In this instance, however, it is used more in the sense of "Japanese-Americans." The week-long celebration includes the coronation of a Nisei Week Queen, a parade, street dancing, exhibitions of martial arts, the tea ceremony, calligraphy, and other cultural forms. Traditional

Japanese foods such as yaki-soba, sushi, sashimi and tempura are a popular part of the program.

The South/Southwest

Southern governors and businessmen are taking extraordinary advantage of their reputation for hospitality to woo Japanese investors. The southern traditions of florid oratory, pomp, ceremony, good food, and whiskey are something the Japanese feel very much at home with. The southern penchant for establishing a solid personal bond with business partners aligns perfectly with Japanese behavior.

In fact, southern politicians and businessmen, who have very long memories, are not above reminding the Japanese that they too were defeated in a war with "Northern U.S.A." and therefore have even more in common with the Japanese than with the "greedy, money-grubbing" northerners.

As a further indication of the way southerners present themselves to the Japanese, *Asia Wall Street Journal* correspondent Bradley K. Martin quotes Bill Kenney, a member of the Development Authority of Cobb County in Georgia, as repeating a saying his father passed along to him: "A northern worker doesn't care how you treat him as long as you pay him well. A southern worker doesn't care what you pay him as long as you treat him well." This is also an attitude the Japanese understand and appreciate.

Martin quotes Norishige Hasegawa, retired chairman of Sumitomo Chemical Co., as saying, "The people in the southern region [of the U.S.] are very kind, as symbolized by the expression 'Southern Hospitality,' and furthermore they are very diligent and respectable"—characteristics the Japanese claim for themselves.

Martin comments on how other Japanese businessmen say they and their families "fit" into southern communities, where the personal touch often comes before profit, and human relations are at the forefront of all business.

While these cultural factors are important to the Japanese, there are also a number of practical economic factors that draw them south of the Mason-Dixon line, including lower wages, lower land and cost of living prices, and better tax advantages.

Of course, "Yankee" businessmen also should be aware of the importance of establishing a solid personal bond with any Japanese they would like to do business with.

Georgia is a typical example of the southern states that have welcomed Japanese investment and Japanese influence. There are presently some 120 Japanese companies operating in the state, employing over 4,000 Americans. YKK, the huge Japanese zipper manufacturer, spent $100 million to expand its Macon plant in 1984–85. At any one time, there are some 4,000 Japanese nationals residing in Georgia.

Besides a Japanese-language school that serves the Japanese community, Japanese-language courses are available for Americans at Brenau College. The Japan-American Society of Georgia has a large membership that is active in promoting a deeper knowledge and appreciation of the arts, industry, culture, and political and social systems of Japan. Besides a growing number of Japanese restaurants and groceries, Georgians are also able to study Japanese gardening, calligraphy, ninjutsu, flower arranging, craftsmanship, and *go* (a chess-like game that originated in China).

In 1973, then Georgia Governor George Busbee and several local businessmen joined with some 10 senior executives of leading Japanese companies to establish the U.S. Southeast/ Japan Association, consisting of the seven states of Georgia, Alabama, Florida, North Carolina, South Carolina, Tennessee, and Virginia. This organization has been instrumental in bringing many other Japanese companies to these states.

Virtually all of the Japanese companies in Georgia are deeply involved in maintaining good relations with their local communities. One example, recounted by Day Lancaster, managing director of Georgia's trade and industry office in Tokyo, is that of Maxell America, a tape manufacturer. Hideo Ogino, president and plant manager, has a photograph of every one of his employees on his office wall to help him remember their faces and names. He also sponsors a monthly party for employees celebrating their birthdays during the month. The company cosponsors an annual spring festival centered on the blossoming of 500 cherry trees that Maxell donated to the city.

Another example (cited by Lancaster) of the willingness of Japanese corporations to invest not only their money, but their time and energy, in promoting the welfare of local communities, involved the Tokai Corporation, Japan's largest manufacturer of disposable lighters. The company had been providing Atlanta's Scripto Inc. with disposable lighters for eight years, during which Scripto went through several changes of owner-ship. Finally, when the company came up for sale again, Tokai bought it in order to stabilize the management. Following the purchase, Tokai invited not only state and city officials, but the entire work force of Scripto, some 600 people, to a reception.

In 1983, Georgia Tech and Nissho Iwai, a major Japanese trading company, signed an agreement covering 30 areas of technology being researched at Georgia Tech and offered to Japanese clients by Nissho—the first agreement of its kind be-tween an American university and a Japanese trading company.

In the Phoenix, Arizona, area, where there are only about 2,000 Japanese-Americans and Japanese nationals combined, activities related to spreading knowledge about Japan—and therefore Japanese influence—is surprising. In 1985, Arizona State University, in collaboration with the Japan-American Society of Phoenix and several other organizations, sponsored a three-month-long program called Behind The Mask: A Cultural Exploration of Japan, which included lectures, films, symposia, performances, exhibits, and a festival.

HAWAII, ETC.

Guam, the U.S.'s westernmost Pacific outpost, is much closer to Japan than it is to the United States, and this proximity is reflected in the amount of Japanese influence on the island. Only a few hours' flying time from Japan's major population centers, yet offering the standard attractions of the tropical island vacationland, Guam is a favorite destination of Japanese tourists, who represent 80 percent of the island's 200,000-plus visitors each year.

There are well over a thousand Japanese nationals living on Guam—mostly businessmen and their families and employees of Japanese companies—with their own Japanese-language school. Courses in Japanese are also taught at the University of Guam, the Guam Community College, the International Business College, and Western Pacific Business College.

Japanese nationals are active in both men's and women's organizations, including the Lions Club, Rotary Club, Kiwanis Club, Guam Chamber of Commerce, and the Guam Business and Professional Women's Club. Guam's cable television station airs four hours of Japanese programs daily.

Guam's economy is more closely linked with that of Japan than any part of America. Because of the strong U.S. military presence on the island, however, and the virtual segregation of visiting Japanese tourists to the hotels and beach areas, there is substantially less social and cultural influence than might be expected—much less than in Hawaii, for example, where Japanese-Americans make up a substantial percentage of the overall population and are an integral part of the social and cultural life of Hawaii.

In fact, Japanese influence in the United States is strongest in Hawaii, where approximately one-fourth of the population is of Japanese ancestry, the number of resident Japanese nationals in comparison to the total population is the highest in the country, and Japanese-owned businesses are a significant factor in Hawaii's economy. Besides the nearly one-quarter of a million Japanese-Americans who live in Hawaii, some 15,000 to 20,000 Japanese nationals make their homes in the state. (Since the law requiring aliens to report their addresses annually was repealed in 1981, data on the exact number of Japanese nationals living in Hawaii is not available.)

Japanese Immigration

The first Japanese immigrants arrived in Hawaii in 1868. They were a group of 153 people recruited to work on Hawaii's sugar plantations by Eugene M. Van Reed, the Hawaiian consul in Yokohama. Reed somehow managed to obtained 300 passports from the Tokugawa Shogunate just before it fell. When the Shogunate was replaced, the new Meiji government confiscated the passports and banned all travel to Hawaii.

Reed was obviously a resourceful fellow, however, and succeeded in smuggling the group of 153 workers aboard the English vessel *Sciot*, which immediately sailed for Honolulu. None of these workers had any experience in working in cane fields. Many of them could not endure the hard work and appealed to the Japanese government to allow them to return to Japan. The Meiji government sent a mission to Hawaii to discuss the affair and eventually agreed to pay the expenses of the immigrants wanting to return home. Some 40 of them accepted the offer.

Following this debacle, the Japanese government was reluctant to allow any more people to emigrate to Hawaii, but reached an agreement with the government of Hawaii in 1884 and thereafter encouraged emigration to the islands. This agreement was formalized in 1886, and officially supervised emigration was to continue until 1924. The first group of government-supervised immigrants embarked on January 27, 1885, when 944 Japanese boarded the *City of Tokio* in Yokohama and arrived in Honolulu on February 8.

Although Hawaii was annexed by the United States in 1898, the influx of Japanese immigrants continued until 1924, when Congress passed an act prohibiting Japanese immigration to the U.S.

Some 90,000 of the more than 200,000 Japanese-Americans who live in Hawaii today still speak the Japanese language in their own homes. Around 3,000 do not speak any English at all. Some 15,000 speak only a little English, and another 25,000 speak English only fairly well. Every year nearly one million Japanese tourists visit Hawaii.

Japanese Investment

Japanese influence is visible and felt in virtually every area of life in Hawaii, from accessories and art to food and footwear. Japanese-Americans are prominent in politics, the professions, and business. In the minds of many, it is in the business area that the Japanization of Hawaii has made the most progress. The first Japanese investment in Hawaii occurred in 1959 when the Shirokiya Department Store, a subsidiary of the huge Tokyu Corporation, opened a branch in the Ala Moana Shopping Center.

The next Japanese company to invest in Hawaii was the *Shizuoka Shimbun* (Newspaper) Co., which bought out the *Hawaii Hochi Newspaper* in 1962. This was followed in 1962 by the construction of the Kaimana Beach Hotel (now the New Otani Beach Hotel) and by the purchase of the famed Princess Kaiulani Hotel on Waikiki, along with the equally famous Moana and Surfrider hotels, by Kokusai Kogyo Co. in 1963.

The first Japanese-owned restaurant in Hawaii, the Furusato, opened in 1964.

The next major Japanese investment in Hawaii did not take place until 1969, when Kokusai Kogyo built a new, 430-room Surfrider Hotel and turned the original Surfrider into the Ocean Lanai wing of the Moana Hotel. Since then, the number and value of Japanese investments in Hawaii has grown steadily.

There are presently over 100 major Japanese-owned properties and businesses in Hawaii. Among the Hawaiian businesses and properties that are totally or primarily owned by Japanese interests are the Sheraton-Kauai Hotel, the Francis Brown Golf Course, In-Flight Catering Company, the Okadaya retail stores, Hawaiian Regent Hotel, Pearl City Tavern, Hilo Hotel, Hawaiian Country Club, Hanalei Plantation Hotel, McInerny Department Stores, Park Shore Hotel, Kahuku Agricultural Co., Breakers Hotel, the Sheraton-Waikiki Hotel, Royal Hawaiian Hotel, Sheraton Maui Hotel, Pearl Country Club, and Pacific Guardian Life Insurance Co., plus numerous condominiums, choice acreage and lots, office buildings, other restaurants and hotels, the Ala Moana Shopping Center, and private estate homes.

The Japanese Future

Given the central Pacific location of Hawaii, the presence of large numbers of Japanese-Americans, and the generally positive attitude toward Japanese investments in the islands, it seems safe to predict that the Japanization of Hawaii will proceed at a far more rapid pace than it will in Mainland USA.

In 1985, Dorothy Ochiai Hazama and Jane Okamoto Komeji, both Nisei (second generation) Japanese-Americans and both schoolteachers, published a book entitled *Okage Sama De: The Japanese in Hawaii,* which tells the saga of how the first Japanese came to Hawaii and their struggles over the years, in the face of prejudice and discrimination, to become a part of the Hawaiian community—and how, in the process, they developed a deep love and appreciation for Hawaii as their homeland. The title of the book, *Okage Sama De*, is a special phrase used to express appreciation and means something like "Thanks to you."

Hawaii is already a favorite retirement place for Americans who have spent years in Japan, developed a deep affinity for many aspects of Japanese culture, and want to continue enjoying some of the best of both worlds. Many students of the Japanese language are also finding it practical to at least begin their studies in Honolulu.

The Japan-American Institute of Management Science in Honolulu, founded in 1972, offers a master's degree in Japanese business studies. Earlier, the Institute offered a certificate of graduation based on a 9-month program that included the Japanese language and culture and a four-month-long internship in Japan. When the school first opened, it had difficulty recruiting students. Now there is a waiting list.

Back in mainland U.S., other schools are adding Japanese programs or expanding their old ones. Temple University in Philadelphia opened a branch campus in Japan in 1982 and offers an MBA program there. The University of Michigan offers graduate students a three-year master's program in Japanese business administration. Business students at Washington and Lee University may study the Japanese language and East Asian history.

All these new and expanded programs are moves in the right direction, but we have a long way to go. In 1983, there were approximately 14,000 Japanese students studying in the United States, compared with 276 American students officially known to be studying in Japan.

It was not until the late 1970s and early 1980s that individual American states began recognizing that they could not depend on the federal government to solve the country's trade problems with Japan. One by one, they began picking up on the idea of opening their own trade-promotion offices in Tokyo. Now approximately half of the 50 American states have offices there.

Competition among the states for Japanese investment is fierce and growing, not only in Tokyo but in the U.S. as well. One of the many approaches here: The state of Indiana set up a Japanese-language school for the children of Japanese businessmen in Indianapolis.

At this writing, there are still a few states with less than half a dozen Japanese companies or none at all (the Dakotas, Wyoming, Utah, Delaware, New Mexico, Montana, Rhode Island), but there are no areas in the United States that are unaffected by Japanese influence.

Chapter IV

The Japanese Are Here!

J apanese companies are opening new sales, marketing, or manufacturing operations in the U.S. almost daily. Virtually every issue of The *Asian Wall Street Journal* carries from one to five or six announcements of such openings. Japanese companies are also continuing to buy American companies of all kinds—totally or in part. On the day of this writing, for example, Nippon Kokan announced that it had agreed to purchase half interest in National Steel Corporation, the sixth largest steel producer in the U.S.

On a single page in a current edition of *Nihon Keizai Shimbun* (*Japan Economic Journal*), six of the eight stories deal with the expansion of Japanese companies into the U.S.: "Mitsui & Co. Acquires California Marketer of Dairy Cow Feedstuffs"; "Toray Has Eye on U.S. Contact Lens Market"; "Japan Trading House to sell Pilot-Training System Designed in U.S."; Yamaha Selling Boat Motors in U.S. Under Its Own Name"; "Komatsu Ltd. Plans Construction-Gear Production in the U.S."; "U.S.-Japan Thermal Power Link."

In a later issue: "Nissho Iwai Buying Shares of U.S. Peripheral Company"; "Hitachi to Build Car Parts in Kentucky"; "Fujisawa Pharmaceutical Co. Buys into Lymphomed Inc. for $26.3 million." The list grows and grows, and no one knows how far it will go or how much is too much.

Japan now supplies the United States with around 25 percent of its automobiles (a figure that would undoubtedly shoot upward if it were not for negotiated political restraints), 90 percent of its motorcycles, over 50 percent of its watches and recording equipment, and 20 to 30 percent of numerous other products.

In 1985, Japan's export of robots to the U.S. surged 50 percent and accounted for approximately the same percentage of robot sales in the U.S. With the Matsushita Group, Japan's largest manufacturing conglomerate, joining other Japanese robot makers in all-out assault on the American robot market, the Japanese are likely to dominate this market for the foreseeable future.

At present, all U.S. robot manufacturers, with the exception of Cincinnati Milacron Inc., are using Japanese companies as subcontractors—and that firm is expected to begin importing robots from foreign makers. Experts in the field say that Japan's industrial robot makers do not have the technological edge on U.S. makers but that the robots they produce are less complicated and less expensive and have a high-quality image.

In other areas of robotics, the Japanese are on the leading edge. Another of the more interesting developments in 1985 was the introduction of a humanoid-type robot by Professor Ochiro Kato of Waseda University, called WL10RD, which might be nicknamed "Willard."

What makes Willard stand out is that "he" can walk like a human being at approximately the same speed as humans. The 58-inch-high robot has jointed legs that allow it to take humanlike strides, negotiate gentle slopes, and go up and down stairs. Later generations of Willard will undoubtedly master the art of walking and performing other humanlike actions and have humanoid characteristics that are now seen only in movies.

Another specific area in which the impact of Japanese influence has been significant is research on so-called ballistic transistors, which are expected to emerge soon from research on high electron-mobility transistors, or "HEMTS," and which are expected to revolutionize computer design. Stated James V. DiLorenzo, head of Bell Lab's gallium arsenide research: "Nobody in the U.S. comes close to Japan's prowess in fabricating integrated circuits from HEMT materials."

THE GROWING PRESENCE

Commenting on the effects of Japanese competition on American industry, a ranking executive in a major U.S. corporation said: "I am in regular contact with many of the largest firms in America. It is striking as one is aware almost immediately upon meeting the management at any level in these firms of its state of mobilization in the face of Japanese competition.

"In those companies lacking this mobilization, the approach to the customer is often one of arrogance, 'take it or leave it.' One such supplier, a major U.S. chemical company with revenue in excess of $30 billion a year, minimizes its exposure to the Japanese threat to its markets. When probed about the basic research in new materials that is being done in Japan, the response is one of either ignorance or indifference. While this attitude may be understandable in light of this company's control of its headquarters town and maybe state, one wonders if the situation will be the same five years from now. Using licenses with this and other U.S. companies as a starting point, Japanese scientists are planning to dominate the world market in fine chemicals by the early 1990s."

This commentator added that one major U.S. computer manufacturer with lucrative license arrangements with NEC and Toshiba during the 1960s and 1970's was placed in the position of having to buy back improved designs of the very systems it had licensed to its Japanese partners. In one case, the repurchase was forced by the threat of the Japanese company selling the improved computer system to one of the firm's major U.S. customers.

Among the American companies that are in a state of war with Japanese competition, the integrated circuit manufacturers are the most aggressive, says the same commentator. "Without fail, within 30 minutes of arriving at one of these companies someone will say, 'We'll bring this device on the market before Hitachi,' or 'Our quality is 20 percent better than NEC,' or even 'We know you are buying this model from Toshiba and we want that business.'

"A number of U.S.I.C. vendors are willing to enter into constraining, long-term relationships with major customers to establish loyalty and gain an edge over their Japanese competition. The U.S. customers of U.S.-manufactured chips are enjoying major improvements in quality, delivery, and price as a result of this pressure. During a recent visit I made to a Silicon Valley supplier, the first level marketing administration people and production management people spent an hour giving me glowing reports of their factory's latest quality improvements, comparing their performance, measured in parts defective per million, with those of major Japanese vendors.

"The seriousness with which IBM has taken the Japanese threat has been documented in two *Fortune* articles in the past year. The first article discusses the $10 billion investment in plant and equipment IBM has made to be a lower-cost supplier of computer equipment than the Japanese. The second article exposes the dichotomy between IBM as a too-aggressive competitor in the U.S. computer market and a national flagship in the combat against the threat of Japanese domination of the industry.

"In a recent visit to the John Deere Tractor Factory in Waterloo, Iowa, I saw firsthand the effect of mobilization on this major farm and construction equipment manufacturer. The company spent $1.5 billion to completely revise its factories and design capability in the face of Japanese competition. Such major advances as robots, modular construction, automated material handling, just-in-time flows, group parts technology, and employee involvement were evident in abundance. Even though the farm equipment industry is in a decline at present, this factory, operating at much less than 100 percent capacity, is making a profit because of the modern techniques in place."

J. F. Lardner, vice president of manufacturing development at Deere, was recently quoted in *Manufacturing Engineering* as saying, "Faced with increasingly successful offshore competition and sharp declines in shares of the world markets, U.S. managers are beginning to take a hard look at the need to achieve superior manufacturing performance in order to guarantee survival.

"This management concern represents an important change from the time when American companies dominated world markets for manufactured goods. From the early 1950s until the latter half of the 1970s, there was little reason to believe that U.S. manufacturing did not represent a standard of manufacturing performance unequaled in the world. However, events of the last several years have shaken this belief, and today manufacturing is struggling to establish standards by which superior manufacturing performance can be measured in a world of global competition.

"Based on what we are learning from this new group of competitors, I am convinced many of the measurements used to judge manufacturing performance in the past 30 years need to be altered or perhaps abandoned. This will not be an easy task."

A Conversion Story

Along this same line, Paul M. Dick, director of materials management for Honeywell Inc.'s large computer product division in Phoenix, Arizona, said: "Significant changes are taking place in our facility here in Phoenix because of the double-edged thrust of the Japanese. On the one hand, the effect of Japan's competitive pressure on our markets, directly and indirectly, as our U.S. competition (IBM) reacts with higher quality and higher performance, is to force a new look at our own internal product offerings. On the other hand, superior Japanese techniques can be copied and even improved on if we have the humility to admit we need new thinking.

"Some of these recent changes include:

1. The initiation of a corporate-wide quality program involving every employee in marketing, engineering, manufacturing, and field support. Early results are being seen as quality improvement teams are working on long overlooked systemic problems. New efforts at group recognition are encouraging the identification of employees with the success of the enterprise.

2. The presentation of daylong seminars to 300 engineers and managers on Japanese manufacturing techniques by Dr. Richard Schonberger, author in this field and a leader in promulgating new thinking in production technology. Videotapes of this session are being used to teach courses in these techniques throughout the corporation.

3. The promotion of a vendor partnership program with the key division suppliers, linking their management and technical people with their counterparts in our local division. New relationships permit material releases without purchase orders, dock-to-dock material flow without incoming inspection, just-in-time delivery of parts—all characteristic of the Japanese customer-vendor networks.

4. The acceptance of the 'new' idea that inventory buffers are bad, unnecessary, and hide latent problems and that a factory can be run with much less material than conventional

thinking would permit. This is having an impact on plant layout, organization structure, stockroom sizes, production scheduling systems, internal quality requirements, and, most importantly, the reduced time to service a customer's order."

Dick summed up by saying, "It is clear to thinking managers that the double-edged Japanese sword is cutting out the fat that we have allowed to accumulate and is accelerating the changes that modern computer and manufacturing technologies have facilitated."

Two American Heroes

Lee Iacocca became an American hero because of his success with Chrysler in the face of serious Japanese competition. He owes his success to the example presented to him by the Japanese—he emulated many of the production techniques of Japanese automobile manufacturers—and to the fact that Americans responded favorably to his appeal to patriotism.

However, I believe that Donald Burr, the founder and president of People Express Airlines, is a greater hero. He started with almost nothing and in four years built one of the largest U.S. airlines, with over 4,000 employees and annual sales in excess of $1 billion.

Burr accomplished this astounding feat by out-Japanizing the Japanese. He went way beyond the Japanese concept that the people (employees) are the enterprise, that they provide the management with advice and help, that they have a lifelong stake in the company, that they should love their company and their work, that they should be loyal to the company unto death, and that self-determination and voluntary cooperation are the essence of management.

Burr has done his best to eliminate hierarchy within the ranks of the employees of People Express Airlines—something that is dear to the hearts of the Japanese and so much a part of their culture that it is difficult to imagine them without it. By this, he has gone so far beyond any existing enterprise system that he is virtually all alone.

In effect, Burr has created what could very well be described as the ideal company—one that is almost totally people-oriented, that is by and for people. His phenomenal success in such a short period of time is proof that his system works—at least in the airline business. The irony is, however, that many people consider his success a complete fluke. Even some of his own employees don't like the system and are trying to change it. They cannot stand the idea of equality and the sense of freedom that exist in the company. They want hierarchy, specialization, and explicit rules and regulations.

Despite his success, Burr describes himself as an unhappy, frustrated man because he has to fight so hard to make his workers understand and accept the opportunities they have as employees of People Express Airlines. Burr's total system would not be appropriate for all types of business, but for many companies it could be a harbinger of things to come.

Japan's business world is filled with men who are known as Confucian-style authoritarians in their approach to management—as tough as Marine drill sergeants but with a strongly paternalistic attitude toward their employees. The closest thing the U.S. has to a Confucian businessman would probably be Don Oberg, owner and president of Oberg Industries Inc., a tool and die manufacturer in Freeport, Pennsylvania.

As profiled by writer Donna Fenn in *Inc.*, Oberg comes across as a benevolent dictator who would fit perfectly into the Japanese scheme of things, with similar success.

Fenn writes that Oberg works his employees 50 hours a week, gives them only 15 minutes for lunch, and does not tolerate idle chitchat or dirty floors or T-shirts or blue jeans or beards or long hair. Most new employees have to spend one or two months working in maintenance as janitors. Yet the company has a long waiting list of people who would like to work there.

Like the Japanese, Oberg has signs outside and inside his spic-and-span plant. Among them: Please clean your feet, dirt is our biggest enemy. If it's almost right, it's wrong. The biggest room in our company is the room for improvement.

Oberg keeps extra signs in his office and gives them to visitors.

Before Oberg hires prospective workers, they have to go through a daylong psychological testing process to see if they can stand the stress of working in such an intense atmosphere on precision products. Machinists must pass difficult written examinations.

In addition to Oberg's disciplinarian approach to management, he also charges from 5 to 10 percent more for his products than other manufacturers in the same industry. How does he get by with working his employees so hard and charging more for his products? He pays his employees well, and they make the highest quality tool and die products in the industry.

"Oberg is one of the few companies that has out-Japanesed the Japanese," says Myron Tribus, director of the Center for Advanced Engineering Study at Massachusetts Institute of Technology. "The Japanese know that quality is the way you solve problems. When you strive for quality, all other things fall in line. Oberg instinctively understood this from the beginning and made it his practice."

Just like larger Japanese companies, Oberg puts his employees through a rigorous on-the-job training program, molding them into a disciplined, proud, and elite group. Just like the Japanese, he has visited factories all over the world in search of ideas to incorporate into his own company.

Unlike the Japanese, however, Oberg does not have the total support of all his managers, whom he frequently bypasses when he sees a problem somewhere. Over the years, he has lost a number of key managers who could not or would not put up with his style of management. His major weakness, notes the *Inc.* article, is his inability or failure to communicate with his managers and convince them of the rightness of his obsession with cleanliness, efficiency, innovation, and quality.

In other American companies that have adopted Japanese-style management practices, the major obstacle—when there is one—is invariably managers who do not understand or approve of the changes. The challenge to top management, of course, is educational. They must reeducate their key employees in an ongoing process that includes a new way of thinking about management, employees, and their mutual responsibilities.

Japanese Outreach

The Japanese government, Japanese industrial associations, and private Japanese companies have been carrying on intensive public relations campaigns in the U.S. for many years. In earlier years, the primary aim of the various agencies and offices set up by the Japanese, primarily in Washington, D.C., was to keep informed on political trends in the U.S. and to lobby for or against the passage of bills that they felt might be detrimental to Japan's trade with the U.S.

In the early 1980s, some of the industrial associations began taking a more grass-roots approach to their PR and lobbying activities in the U.S., enlisting the help of their dealers and distributorships around the country. A leader in this effort was the Keizai Koho Center (Economics Information Center), an arm of Japan's Federation of Economic Organizations (Keidan-ren), which is charged with the responsibility for telling Japan's economic story abroad and persuading both the public and private sectors to be more understanding and sympathetic toward Japan's position.

Japan's Consulate General of New York operates a mobile outreach program to bring speakers, films, and printed materials to teachers who want their students to learn something about Japan. Topics discussed run the gamut from politics to life-styles.

Japanese companies station far more employees in the U.S. than American companies do in Japan. There are presently some 75,000 Japanese businessmen living in the United States, with over 150,000 family members, while there are around 9,500 Americans in Japan representing U.S. companies. As of mid-1985, there were 348 Japanese-American joint venture companies in the U.S. in which the Japanese investment was over 50 percent. Altogether, these firms employed a total of 68,600 people, including the Japanese staff.

The larger Japanese manufacturing companies also dispatch several thousand employees abroad each year on "fact-finding" trips. NEC, for example, sends around 8,000 people abroad each year. Some 6,000 Toshiba employees make trips abroad each year, and so on. Every year, the Japan Productivity Center sends some 50 study teams overseas to visit foreign research institutes, manufacturers, and other organizations.

Beginning in the 1960s, major Japanese companies began to systematically send promising young executives to the American Graduate School of International Management in Glendale, Arizona, to Harvard Business School, and to other American schools to study business administration. In my own classes at AGSIM, where I lectured on doing business in Japan, during the mid-1970s, up to one-fourth of my students were young Japanese businessmen on assignment from their companies!

Mitsubishi Corporation and Nomura Securities were pioneers in sending employees to the U.S. for MBAs. Nomura sends 30 employees abroad to study for MBAs each year at a current cost of 450 million yen. Some 40 percent of Nomura's international staff have MBAs from American or European universities.

I am not aware of a single American ever being sent to Japan or to a Japanese university by an American company solely to study the art of doing business in Japan. Japanese industry, on the other hand, has the benefit of tens of thousands of Japanese executives who have received years of training at American universities at company expense!

The typical American company interested in doing business in Japan either downplays or totally ignores the idea of employing someone with Japan experience to tackle the job. The idea of their sending their own personnel to Japan for study would likely be greeted by a big horselaugh. Their biggest fear, of course, would be that as soon as the employee finished the training, he or she would quit the sponsoring company and go with another firm.

In 1985, several of Japan's leading trading companies announced drastic changes in their personnel policies that would result in their hiring more Americans and eventually make it possible for non-Japanese to reach high executive positions. Sumitomo Corporation said it was abandoning its policy of Japanese-style personnel management in its foreign subsidiaries and would hereafter adapt its hiring and promotion practices to local customs. Nissho Iwai Corporation said it would recruit college graduates as candidates for executive posts in countries where it has subsidiaries.

These changes, extraordinary for Japanese companies, are being "forced" on the trading companies because it is getting more costly for them to maintain Japanese personnel abroad, the traditional system of restricting foreign employees to low-level management positions prevents the companies from attracting more qualified employees, and the Japanese are beginning to feel and react to foreign pressure to internationalize their overseas subsidiaries.

The changes will be slow in coming, however, with very little impact for at least a decade. In the meantime, most Japanese companies with large numbers of employees stationed abroad will probably extend the length of stay of key personnel to cut down on costs and get more benefit out of their experience.

THE AMAZING AUTO AFFAIR

The Japanese were late in developing an automobile manufacturing industry. Wheeled carts for transporting goods and members of the Imperial family were in use in Japan in ancient times. There was an officer in charge of royal carts at the Imperial Court when the great historical chronicle *Nihon Shoki* was published in 720 A.D. The first modern auto was imported into Japan in 1897 by a foreign resident. The first car was manufactured there in 1904 by a man named Torao Yamaha in Okayama Prefecture. World War I provided the primary impetus for the development of an auto industry after the Japanese had observed the role that trucks and other vehicles played in war.

However, the arrival in Japan of the Ford Motor Company in 1925 and General Motors in 1926, with large assembly plants, resulted in a lag in the development of Japanese-owned automobile companies. In 1931, the Japanese government got involved in promoting the design and production of automobiles by Japanese companies. In 1936, the government passed an Automobile Production Enterprise Law to support large-scale auto production in the country. Ford and General Motors were forced to close their operations in Japan just before the outbreak of World War II. Virtually all the Japan-owned auto manufacturing facilities were destroyed by American bombing raids during the war.

When the first made-in-Japan automobiles were imported into the United States in the late 1950s, the American automobile industry was asleep at the wheel and took no special notice of this historic event. The American automobile moguls smiled indulgently at these tiny minnows in their big ocean.

The years passed quickly. The trickle of Japanese cars into the U.S. grew into a stream. American automobile manufacturers, workers, and many politicians grumbled about "cheap labor" and unfair government tactics and continued full speed down a narrowing primrose highway that was littered with potholes.

American automobile manufactures continued to argue that Americans were big-car lovers and would soon stop flirting with little Japanese imports, buy a large, comfortable American-made car, and settle down.

The quality of American-made cars, on a steep slide for several years, continued to deteriorate. Management treated labor like a necessary evil and workers as drones. Labor regarded management as the devil incarnate and continued to demand higher and higher wages for less and less work that was becoming shoddier and shoddier.

Like the little engine that could, the Japanese automobile industry kept chugging away, getting bigger, better, and stronger. U.S. automakers began laying off workers and closing plants.

In the 1970s, the stream of Japanese cars into the U.S. became a flood, sending American auto manufacturers reeling and on the verge of a technical knockout. Shocked out of decades of self-induced inefficiency and arrogant smugness, American car makers began emergency measures in an effort to avoid being knocked out of the ring altogether. For the first time in a long time, automakers began looking seriously at what had happened to their productivity and their quality. Many of them made contrite trips to Japan to see if they could learn some of the secrets of Japan's success. Some of them began to hedge their future by buying into or increasing their holdings in Japanese companies, along with forming production and marketing alliances with Japanese auto manufacturers in the U.S. Chrysler bought into Mitsubishi motors in 1971. GM tied up with Isuzu Motors the same year and with Mazda in 1975, Suzuki in 1981, and Toyota in 1983. In 1985, General Motors boosted its stake in Isuzu Motors from 34.2 percent to 38.6 percent "to strengthen their ties and meet growing international competition." Rumors have it that GM may increase its ownership of Isuzu to 41 percent.

By 1983, a number of American car makers had decided to move part of their manufacturing process out of the U.S., while Japanese companies significantly expanded their American manufacturing and sales operations and continued to plan for further growth. Even the great American entrepreneur Lee Iococca remarked at this time, "We're a Colony again—this time of Japan!"

"Japan Inc."

U.S. News & World Report recently referred to "Japan Inc." as the fourth largest automobile manufacturer in the United States. All of Japan's top four automakers—Honda, Toyota, Nissan, and Mazda—have automobile manufacturing operations in the U.S. or are in the process of opening plants. Their projected annual vehicle output is over one million units—at which time they will be employing some 15,000 American workers directly. The sales of Japanese-made car parts in the United States is growing at the rate of 12 to 15 percent a year, as opposed to a growth rate of two to three percent in the American car parts industry.

The impact of Japanese automobile manufacturers in the United States goes far beyond the number of workers they employ directly and indirectly. Far more important is the influence they are having on the thinking and behavior of American automakers and on American unions. Japanese auto companies make changes in their famous management style to fit the American environment, but they get more than they give. In plants that were unionized, they demanded and got more flexibility in union work rules. They were not about to accept the kind of counterproductive union rules that plague American automobile manufacturers. In the joint GM-Toyota factory in Fremont, California, the lowest ranking member of the assembly line has the right to push a red button that stops the whole line if he or she spots a production defect. This is just one aspect of worker participation in what is usually considered a management prerogative in the U.S., and the GM-Toyota "experience" is being watched closely by the rest of the American auto industry. It represents a breakthrough not only for American management, but for American unions as well—and it would not have happened without the Japanese influence in America.

GM's early-1985 announcement that it was setting up an entirely new company called Saturn to produce small automobiles using Japanese techniques was styled as the giant automaker's "boldest plan yet to counter Japanese imports." It was, perhaps, the single most stunning example yet of Japanese influence on American industry. Other announcements by GM in mid-1985 included plans to spend $1.1 billion modernizing and expanding stamping facilities in Marion, Indiana, and a pressed-metal unit in Parma, Ohio—also the result of the rippling effect of Japanese influence.

If the American government had remained on the sidelines and neutral, there is little doubt that Japanese automobile manufacturers would have captured as much as 50 percent of the American car market. As it is, the challenge from Japanese car makers is the single greatest force at play in the American auto industry. If it had not been for this Japanese challenge, the American auto industry would still be driving while half asleep, abusing the American consumer and raping the environment.

The success of Japan's major automobile manufacturers in the U.S. is both conspicuous and significant. Toyota Motor Corporation, Japan's largest auto manufacturer, began its first full year of operation in the United States in 1958. That year, fewer than 300 Toyota cars were sold in the U.S. Today there are some 1,100 Toyota dealerships and distributors in the U.S., employing over 40,000 American workers, with annual sales in excess of 600,000 units.

The annual sales of Toyota Motor Sales (USA) are well above $5 billion, which puts it in the top 65 industrial corporations in America. Each year Toyota's U.S. operations pump nearly $2 billion back into the American economy in the form of payrolls, taxes, purchases, advertising, and promotional activities.

Toyota attributes its phenomenal success in the United States to putting the interests of consumers first—a philosophy that was basically alien to American automakers and workers until they were forced to recognize it by the threat from Japanese automobile manufacturers.

In recognition of its "responsibility to American society," Toyota makes substantial financial contributions to various American organizations and activities each year. These contributions go to schools, research institutes, museums, symphony orchestras, cultural centers, hospitals, the Highway Users Federation, community safety programs, the U.S. Olympic Committee, and so on.

In August 1985, Toyota announced that it would begin producing its own cars in the United States (and Canada) by 1988. Initial plans call for the production of 200,000 mid-sized cars a year. Engines and power trains for the cars will be produced in Japan.

The common sense and vitality now being demonstrated by the American automobile industry is a direct response to competition from Japan, and if the industry is going to survive and prosper, both management and labor are going to have to continue learning lessons from the Japanese.

Japanese cars have been so successful so quickly in the United States that their success has outdistanced the influence of the high-quality service that marked their first years in the U.S. Consumer satisfaction with the American dealers of Japanese cars is now dropping. Only one Japanese auto company made the Top 10 in terms of satisfaction with dealer after service. Toyota came in No. 10, according to J. D. Power & Associates, a California-based marketing-information company specializing in cars.

The huge Japanese ships that were made especially to transport automobiles to the United States might very well be compared to Admiral Perry's "Black Ships" and the enforced opening of Japan to the West in 1853 *by the United States*. The big difference, of course, is that the Japanese ships are welcomed to the United States with open arms and fanfare.

Japanese autos in the U.S. are just the tip of the iceberg. The success of a large number of Japanese companies in the United States is one of the most significant aspects of the Japanization of America. The American subsidiary of Japan's huge trading company, Mitsui & Co., is the third largest exporting company in the United States, but its activities are virtually unknown to the general public. Many Americans are also not aware that Panasonic, National, Sharp, Canon, and many other famous brand names are Japanese.

The American branches of Japan's largest trading companies account for some four percent of all American exports!

More of the Same

Another conspicuous aspect of the growing Japanese presence in the U.S. is advertising, particularly magazine ads and TV commercials. As early as 1961, leading Japanese companies began running an annual special advertising section in *Fortune* magazine. The most recent one featured the ads of 40 ranking Japanese companies that read like a miniature *Who's Who* of Japan's corporate world: NEC, Canon, Mitsubishi, Matsushita, Brother, Hitachi, Toshiba, Sumitomo, Citizen Watch, Hattori Seiko (world's largest watchmaker), Fujitsu, Mitsui, Nomura Securities, Bridgestone, etc.

Japanese influence is having a profound effect on some pharmaceutical, candy, and gum manufacturing companies. One example: In the March 4, 1985, issue of *Fortune*, writer Steven Flax noted that techniques borrowed from Japanese automaking companies and introduced to Warner-Lambert Co. by consultant James Harbour were saving that company $300 million a year (despite the fact that many managers in the firm were resisting the changes).

What Harbour helped Warner-Lambert do was use Japanese techniques to tighten up control of the production process, giving the company far greater product reliability and allowing it to reduce its inventory by 18 percent; reduce the lead time for purchasing materials and the time needed for manufacturing; improve inspection process techniques; and, with these improvements, begin investing in new technology.

Harley-Davidson, the company that was long synonymous with motorcycles, is another outstanding example of an American company that would have failed had it not taken a crash course in the Japanese way of doing things and applied the techniques to its operation (and had not the U.S. government slapped heavy duties on imported large motorcycles to give it mouth-to-mouth resuscitation).

As in so many cases with American companies, Harley-Davidson was on the brink of disaster before it turned to its Japanese competitors for lessons. Even then, 13 of its top executives had to buy the company and take it private before they could steer it out of the ever-deepening rut that was leading it to ruin. Before the changeover, it took the company 72 days to make a frame. After adapting several Japanese production techniques, it got the process down to two days.

One of the key Japanese techniques adapted by Harley-Davidson was Toyota's famous just-in-time inventory system. The first year, they saved $22 million in inventory costs and dramatically cut the lead times. Before the switch to Japanese methods, absenteeism was rampant at the company, and 50 percent of the motorcycles coming off the line at the York plant had defects. Now the defective rate is said to be down to one percent.

A significant sign of the rebirth of the company: The California Highway Patrol began buying Harley-Davidson motorcycles again in 1985, after 10 years of using Japanese-made machines. Other boosters of the renovated cycles include the Hell's Angels.

CHAPTER V

The Japanese Way

Our social system has produced one of the most violent and abusive societies on the planet. Child abuse, wife-beating, sex-related crimes, senseless murders, thievery, and other crimes resulting from a general breakdown in ethics and morality are commonplace.

The cultural problems in the United States are particularly evidenced by the growing number and savagery of mass murders. The shooting of nearly 50 innocent people by a crazed man at a restaurant and the murder and mayhem committed by a man who deliberately drove his car at high speed down a crowded sidewalk are just two of the more shocking examples of the syndrome.

The problem is so deeply rooted in the fabric of American society—in the whole economic, social, and political morass— that there are no single answers, no simple solutions. However, there is some evidence that the continuing misunderstanding, misuse, and abuse of human sexuality is at the root of most social violence.*

In Japan, on the other hand, most personal violence has traditionally been internalized. When an individual became severely demoralized or depressed, he or she committed suicide. Crazed people striking out at innocent bystanders is still very

*See *Eros' Revenge—Brave New World of American Sex* by Boye De Mente.

rare in Japan, although there are occasional mass murders by poisoning and such isolated incidents as terrorist attacks by members of tiny, fanatical political groups.

The American way of violence is a product of our cultural system. People find it more and more difficult to cope. They lose control and lash out at others in a subhuman rage—then blame society. This accusation may sound irresponsible, but it is right. In the broader context, our system is to blame. Such unexpected outbursts of insanity by people who have led normal lives for many years are not caused by organic problems. They are psychological—and ultimately social in origin.

Years ago, an American doctor who wrote a book on the treatment of mental problems in Japan was astounded to discover that the Japanese insane are almost never violent. Steel doors, iron bars, and physical restraints are seldom, if ever, needed in Japan.

This is still generally true.

Why?

What is it in Japan's culture that causes even the insane to turn their anger inward instead of outward?

Here too, the explanation is found in the total context of the Japanese culture—in the overpowering motivation to maintain harmony in all personal relations, in their emphasis on discipline and respect for authority.

JAPANESE VALUES

The Japanese principle of harmony is religious and philosophical, as well as economic and social. In earlier generations, it was one of the highest laws of the land. Sanctions against anyone who disrupted a carefully prescribed harmony were swift and severe. Still today, *wa* (peace, harmony) is at the foundation of much that is called the Japanese Way, despite the lapses now occurring in schools among adolescent male students and the rowdy behavior of drunken truck drivers.

In pre-1945 Japan, the Way of Wa was built into the structure and guidelines of Japanese society. It began with nursing at the mother's breast and was the main ingredient in all human relations thereafter. Proper relationships between individuals were minutely prescribed. Conformity was not only expected, it was enforced.

During my first years in Japan, I saw numerous situations where I expected to see an argument if not a fistfight. Yet, the people involved would quietly bow to each other and apologize without raising their voices. If the situation was somewhat serious, they would exchange name cards, so the matter could be taken up later and resolved. One of the feudal sanctions that helped keep public squabbles down was the practice of considering both parties equally guilty and punishing both of them. Public good took precedence over personal feelings.

By contrast, we Americans have traditionally been raised on friction, competition, and conflict. Even our Christian God is a violent deity whose hand is perpetually raised, ready to strike us down. We are conditioned from infancy to fight for what we want, to strike at anyone who thwarts us. We are taught from childhood to stand up for our personal, individual rights. We are repeatedly exhorted to grow up, be independent, and take care of ourselves. These are the instincts of the hunter, of a creature who must be able and willing to kill to survive.

Syndicated columnist Ellen Goodman has written eloquently on the psychological ambivalence of American culture. On the one hand, we have a deep-seated awareness that without sharing and togetherness life loses its meaning. Yet, on the other hand, we teach our children to be self-reliant and self-serving. Goodman was echoing the findings of five sociologists who reported in their book *Habits of the Heart* that Americans suffer from such a duality of character that most of them are unable to express themselves except in terms of self, that they simply have no vocabulary of connection, of togetherness. Goodman concluded that we need "a language to describe the values of sharing and the ways joint effort enlarges any enterprise and mutes loneliness."

"Amae"

In trying to understand some of the cultural differences between Americans and Japanese, it is very useful to think of the former as hunters and the latter as farmers. In America, the strong young man has traditionally been the ideal. The man who could run the fastest, shoot the straightest, ride the best, bring home the most meat for the table, and fend off the strongest enemy was often more important to the survival of a family or community than older men. With brawn, skill, and bravery, even a very young man could become a leader.

In Japan, where the overwhelming majority of the population were rice farmers for nearly two thousand years, the most desirable attributes in a leader were the experience and wisdom that come only with age, the suppression of personal desires on behalf of the community, and total cooperation with the group.

A very different cultural influence led Westerners—and especially Americans—to think in terms of the job or the need first and then someone with the ability to do it. In Japan, the people came first, and the job or need came second. This is why American companies identify specific job vacancies and look for people with the qualifications to fill them, while larger Japanese companies generally make no effort at all to match jobs and new employees. They hire young, inexperienced people and then train them to do a variety of jobs as they advance in seniority.

The main building block of Japanese society is a factor called *amae*, which can be translated as selfless love, selfless trust, selfless dependence, first on the mother, then the family, and finally the group—exactly the opposite of the American Way.

We regard such dependence as appropriate only during infancy. As soon as a baby starts to walk, we begin to wean it away from *amae*. How many times have you heard, "Stop acting like a baby! Grow up!"—all aimed at conditioning the young to become independent and act on their own.

In contrast to this, the aim of the Japanese Way is to develop *amae* in all relationships and nurture it continuously so that it becomes both the basis of and the main guideline for behavior—in business, as well as private life. To be sure, even the *amae* found in Japan is not always the ideal of the principle. It is not all selfless. In fact, if not practiced sincerely, it can result in unwanted and unwelcome obligations.

Still, *amae* is a highly sophisticated concept that the Japanese discovered very early in their history, and they have since attempted to make it the foundation of their culture. *Amae* was also discovered in the West ages ago, but having evolved into aggressive hunting societies in which personal independence was the ideal and having fashioned our religions to match our character, we have abandoned it.

Western writer Lafcadio Hearn, who spent the last several years of his life in Japan (1890-1904), was tremendously impressed with living in the great womb of the Japanese Way. In one of his many books, he said living in Japan was like getting a taste of paradise.

Of course, there were blemishes in paradise, but as long as the Japanese were not stirred up and manipulated by their own ultraright military leaders dreaming of empire, the *amae* principle helped make them a unique, totally delightful people.

I strongly recommend that we adopt both the principle and the word *amae*. We need the word because we don't have one to refer to the principle. We need to label the principle in order to understand it clearly and teach it.

The principle itself is nonethnic and nonreligious and is therefore nonthreatening. To those who claim that the *amae* principle is the basis of Christianity and that we don't need to get it from the Japanese, all I can say is, "Look around you! Look at the history of the so-called Christian nations! Look at the religious wars of the past and the present!"

Like the Japanese at the tail end of the Tokugawa era, we need a change. We need to renew our ethical and moral foundations, to restructure our whole social system. I believe the wholesale adoption of many aspects of Japanese culture would help contribute to this renewal, and I'm all for it.

In numerous ways, the United States is still where Japan was some one thousand years ago. The similarities include the growing reluctance of Americans to get involved with neighbors or strangers, emphasizing form and style, instead of content and quality, and allowing the government to dictate our mode of life down to minute details.

Emotion

Mike Lustig, the high school teacher from Bensonhurst, New York, discovered that viewing Japanese television commercials had a significant effect on his students. He explained: "From the very first commercial I showed, the atmosphere of the class changed, especially after the often agitated states created by the American-style high-pressure repetitive messages. Reacting to the variety of moods created by the Japanese commercials, the students sat as if riveted for what seemed to be endless moments. The moods seemed to be sinking in, and all that the first student to break the silence could say was, 'Whew! That was something else!' Other students followed with similar remarks.

"As a result of viewing approximately two dozen commercials, my students concluded (quite remarkably) that Japanese culture was a nonverbal or 'cool' one, a highly technological yet traditional one, a mixed one of East and West, a family-oriented one with a close affinity for nature and house; that Japanese were patient, artistic, and people-oriented, loved children, and were more concerned with images, moods, and subjectivity than a plethora of facts and objectivity."

In the short space of 60 minutes, Lustig's students learned for themselves an important lesson about the connection between attitude and behavior and an important truth about the Japanese: that a basic respect for others is an emotional, not an intellectual, characteristic. The Japanese acknowledge the emotional side of their character and take pride in the emotional content of their culture. Americans, generally speaking, do not. We are conditioned to take an intellectual approach to everything, to suppress our emotions and keep our personal feelings out of the office and the company.

Americans, in fact, are not programmed to be people-sensitive. On the contrary, we are taught and trained to do things by the book and to minimize or ignore the human element. This means, of course, that our whole cultural process is out of order, and we will continue to be at a disadvantage in dealing with the people of other countries, not just Japan, until we re-create our culture according to humanistic principles.

Honesty

Every year in the United States, Americans steal somewhere around $10 billion worth of merchandise from their employers. The amount of time American workers steal from their employers each year is anybody's guess. Theft by professional criminals is also rampant and is valued in the billions of dollars annually. Respect for other people's property and the kind of innate honesty that used to be the hallmark of virtually every man and woman have not disappeared from the American scene, but they are rapidly becoming the exception rather than the rule.

I remember an incident that occurred in Japan some time ago that is still typical of the Japanese, even though their own ethics have been eroded by the Westernization of their society. I spent a night in an inn and left the following morning without my raincoat and without leaving any forwarding address. Two years later I went back to the same inn. The proprietress greeted me in the *genkan* (vestibule).

"Ah, Mr. De Mente! You forgot your raincoat!" she said.

I was amazed that she remembered my name. I was even more surprised when she stepped into a storage area, took my coat out, and handed it to me.

One of the most conspicuous aspects of Japanese society prior to World War II and the replacement of Shintoism and Confucianism with democratic principles was a degree of selflessness and honesty that astounded foreign visitors. This honesty and goodwill often were carried to extremes that Americans would consider foolish.

Another incident that took place back during the Tokugawa period in old Edo (Tokyo) illustrates the degree of honesty that was expected of most Japanese. A man on his way home from work one evening found a money pouch that contained nine *ryo*. Also inside the pouch was the owner's first name. The finder took time off from his own work to search for the owner. After several days of dogged effort, he finally located the man who had lost the money.

When the owner of the money found out how long it had taken the man to find him, he refused to accept the money, saying the finder should keep it for having spent so much of his time in the search. The finder refused to keep the money, saying he had not returned it in the expectation of receiving a reward. The two men got into a loud argument. Finally, the altercation came to the attention of the authorities and the case was taken to court.

In court, both of the men continued to refuse the money. The judge, who was famous for his wisdom in handling personal disputes, settled the case by ordering each of the men to accept three *ryo*, saying that the court would keep the other three *ryo* for the trouble the men had caused.

Honesty is still the norm in Japan and, while it is not an exclusively Japanese trait, it is an example that we need to emulate — which means, of course, that we must have a reformation in our cultural process. One of the reasons for the significant success of Coca-Cola in Japan is the inherent honesty of the Japanese. Coca-Cola (Japan) has over 500,000 vending machines, most of which are located outdoors—something the parent company wouldn't dare to do in the U.S. Weldon Johnson, president of the Japan operation, explains that since Japan is virtually a crime-free country, *they do not have to worry about the machines being vandalized!*

Since ethics must be lived, as well as taught, the challenge is formidable. How about a state religion that has no deities, no organization, and no leaders—only a code of ethics that is taught to every individual from infancy on? This would be something very much like the blend of Shintoism, Buddhism, and Confucianism that makes up the fabric of Japanese culture.

THE PURSUIT OF BEAUTY

American definitions and standards of beauty are not based on any objective formula and tend to be loose and variable. Among most Americans, a serious interest in aesthetics is apt to raise critical comment—and can even get one ostracized from certain groups. It is therefore not surprising to find that there are no commonly held bases for recognizing and appreciating beauty in the West.

In Japan, on the other hand, the main threads of the cultural fabric are pure aesthetics. For more than a thousand years, the Japanese have made the appreciation of beauty a part of their daily lives. It is something they study and practice as part of their being Japanese. The model and standard for beauty is that which is natural or suggested by nature—including what most Westerners would generally describe as ugly.

The Japanese concept of beauty originated in China in the teachings of Lao Tsu, the founder of Taoism, which holds that there is beauty in everything in nature and that it is up to the viewer to see it. The great Tao masters who followed Lao Tsu also taught that it was possible to really appreciate beauty only if a person allowed beauty to permeate and direct his life. Their principle was that until one could make his own thoughts and behavior beautiful, it was sacrilege to approach beauty.

In Japan, this cultural characteristic developed in successive stages within the language, the arts, and handicrafts, finally culminating in the tea ceremony, which was an exercise in pure aestheticism. The nature of beauty as expounded by the greatest tea masters is summed up in the word *shibumi* (the adjectival form is *shibui*), which can be translated as astringent, simple, conservative, rough, elegant, unaffected, etc. *Shibui* beauty is beauty that is in perfect harmony with nature and has a tranquil effect upon the viewer. It suggests serenity, nobility, and quiet luxury. It is a work of art in which all the elements are properly arranged and balanced.

To the Japanese, beauty that is shamelessly displayed becomes vulgar. It must be humble and modest. It is up to the trained taste of the connoisseur to bring it out. Frugality and restraint are both hallmarks of beauty and graceful living.

Most Americans automatically distinguish between the decorative arts, which aim at harmony between beauty and utility, and the fine arts, which are devoted to aesthetic enjoyment. The Japanese commonly mix the two. They see no reason to separate life from art. This accounts for the presence of beauty in every Japanese home. For, no matter how poor or how low on the social ladder, the Japanese family will possess a few pieces of pottery or lacquerware that are works of art.

In *The Way of Tea*, Soetsu Yanagi writes: "The world may abound in different aspects of beauty. The lovely, the powerful, the gay, the smart—all belong to the beautiful. Each person according to his own disposition and environment will feel special affinity to one or another aspect. But when his taste grows more refined, he will necessarily arrive at the beauty that is *shibui*. Beauty cannot rest until it reaches that point."

In practice, a certain color scheme is necessary to produce the *shibui* quality. Combinations of the colors of unpolished gold and silver, ashes, various shades of chestnut or russet, and such natural colors as kelp green and grain chaff are among the most common elements essential for producing the subdued, tranquil effect that is described as *shibui*.

After centuries of exposure to the principles and practices of *shibui* living, the Japanese have developed the ability to recognize and produce the quality almost instinctively. They do not have to strain to judge whether or not something is beautiful.

When the Japanese say that something is beautiful, it is the "soul" of the object they are praising, not the skill or technique that made it. The more human the impression imparted by the object, the deeper their feelings of kinship and pleasure. To the Japanese, an object must be familiar and sympathetic to be beautiful. They hold that it is impossible to admire the truly vain—in man or in his handiwork. They demand humility in both. To be beautiful, an object must lack something which the viewer can add from himself. There must be a "vacuum" which the viewer can enter and fill up to the full measure of his aesthetic ability. In order to accomplish this, the viewer has to cultivate the proper frame of mind. The angry, prejudiced, or frustrated person is in no mood to appreciate beauty.

The ability to perceive and appreciate beauty is not a mechanical skill that once learned need not be exercised. Recognizing this, the Japanese long ago developed customs and ceremonies designed to maintain and strengthen their aesthetic powers. These include organized beauty-viewing parties (of the moon and of cherry and plum blossoms) and the tea ceremony.

Americans can take a quantum leap forward in their cultural development by adopting Japan's *shibui* standard of beauty and learning the principles and practices that are necessary to produce and appreciate it.*

The aspects of refined, graceful living that have been exemplified in Japan for centuries by the tea ceremony are becoming more common in the U.S. and represent an area of influence that can be readily identified and promoted. Of course, the principles involved are not all unique to Japan and are not *Japanese* in any particular sense, but Japan is the only country where they were codified, taught on a mass scale, and made part of the national life-style.

In traditional Japan, one of the ultimate compliments one person could pay another was to describe him or her as a *cha ga aru hito* or "a person who has tea." This meant that the individual, usually through dedicated practice of the tea ceremony and other arts, had achieved a high degree of refinement in his or her behavior, was in tune with the seasons, understood and appreciated true beauty, was sensitive to the emotional

*For additional reading, see *Japanese Secrets of Graceful Living*, by Boye De Mente.

and spiritual needs of others, was free of pretense and arrogance and self-agrandizement, and lived a life filled with grace, goodwill, and quiet pleasure.

The difference between people who "have tea" and those who do not is very obvious and conspicuous to those who know the Japanese Way. There is a serenity and naturalness about people who "have tea" that sets them apart.

If Americans are ever to achieve the quality of life that many of them aspire to, they are going to have to incorporate the tea ceremony or something very much like it into their life-style. Training in the way of tea, which begins early and continues throughout life, would help alleviate many of the social, political, and economic problems that now afflict the United States.

Poetry

Poetry is one of the highest forms of intellectual and artistic expression and is a tangible measure of the mental refinement of an individual. When a significant percentage of the people of a country are avid, practicing poets, it says a lot for their cultural sophistication.

The regular writing of poetry was a widespread phenomenon in Japan by the seventh century A.D. The world's first anthology of poetry was compiled and published in Kyoto, Japan, in the eighth century. Called *Manyoshu* (Ten Thousand Leaves of Grass), this anthology contained nearly 4,000 poems, written over a period of several generations by emperors, high government officials, warriors, priests, craftsmen, and farmers.

In the centuries that followed, poetry writing became an integral part of the life-style of the Japanese, flavoring and influencing the total culture. Many of Japan's greatest heroes are as well remembered for their poetry as for their accomplishments in diplomacy, war, religion, and crafts. This natural penchant for poetry remains a vital force in modern-day Japan, although it has weakened since the introduction of machine industry.

It would be difficult to claim that the traditional Japanese muse has already made itself felt in a significant way in the Unites States, but it is one Japanese speciality that I believe could enhance the quality of American life if the practice of writing poetry, especially the beautiful Japanese haiku, were adopted wholesale.

Fortunately, we have our own homegrown muse that by itself has become something of a national phenomenon since the 1960s. Perhaps as many as 25 percent of all adult Americans have at least tried their hand at poetry at one time or another. There are hundreds of poetry clubs, dozens of state, regional, and national organizations, and numerous journals and other publications featuring poetry. Yet, Americans in general do not regard poetry as a serious or important form of cultural expression.

To the vast majority of Americans (and most publishers), the writing of poetry is a very minor activity of no particular significance. There are few financial rewards and very little prestige or honor for the overwhelming majority of American poets.

I suggest that we take another page from the book of Japan and institute a national poetry contest sponsored by the President, with the winners receiving substantial financial prizes and given national recognition. Furthermore, I believe the writing and appreciation of poetry should be made mandatory in the American school system, beginning with elementary school and continuing through high school.

Some American schools are already moving in this direction, and some have gone well beyond the Japanese approach to poetry. In elementary and high schools in suburbs of Dallas, Texas, American children are often taught how to write haiku as part of an intensive six-week course on Japanese culture, including *kana* (Japanese ideograms) writing, history, and painting.

The ability to appreciate and write poetry is a wonderful test of intelligence, character, personality, and cultural achievement. Of course, poetry can be warped to fit the political or religious ambitions of unscrupulous people, but when it is pursued sincerely for personal enjoyment, it is a sure sign of sensitivity to the human condition and the world at large.

Tsuki-Mi, or "moon-viewing," as an aesthetic practice was already well established in Japan over 1,000 years ago. Places that offered especially beautiful views of the moon were nationally known and moon-viewing platforms or pavilions were built on these sites—some of which are still in use today.

Although considerably diminished by the fast pace and

plastic quality of modern life, moon-viewing is still practiced by many older Japanese. The custom is a simple one. In autumn, when the heat and humidity of the summer have gone and the moon is full, people gather in parks and on knolls, verandas, and specially built platforms to gaze at the moon and compose haiku poetry celebrating its beauty. Drinking and eating specially prepared foods is also part of the pleasure of moon-viewing.

Tsuki-Mi is a delightful custom that helps families and friends communicate with each other by sharing in the appreciation of beauty and the joy of togetherness. It is also a delightful intellectual exercise. Anybody can plan and sponsor a moon-viewing party. The only prerequisite is knowing how to compose haiku-style poetry, so that there really is an intellectual content to the exercise.

A Japanese haiku is always exactly 17 syllables arranged in three lines of five, seven, and five syllables. To create an original haiku in English, you must fashion a sentence of eight, nine, or ten words dealing with nature or life and evoking a sharp, poignant image that distills the essence of the subject.

Crafts

The first Americans to see Japanese handsaws probably laughed and said something like "Dumb Japanese! They can't even make tools right!"

Japanese handsaws and other cutting tools are made to be pulled instead of pushed, cutting on the upstroke instead of the downstroke. These tools, used in Japan for the last thousand and more years, originated in China (and possibly some other Asian countries). As usual, the Japanese made various improvements in them over the centuries.

It is believed by some that Asian craftsmen developed "pull" instead of "push" tools because they habitually worked sitting cross-legged on the floor or ground, a position in which it is easier to control the stroke of a saw or plane on the pull than on the push, and a lot less tiring. I favor the idea that Asians developed pull-tool technology because this allows them to exercise significantly more control over the movement of the tool, and thus cut a straighter line or plane a smoother surface.

Once Western craftsmen get over their culturally biased reaction to pull tools, they often find them superior to the push versions. In fact, Japanese hand-tools have virtually taken over a number of American handicraft industries, such as violin making. The importation of Japanese hand-tools into the U.S. is a multimillion-dollar-a-year business and growing rapidly. There is even a newsletter published by Mahogany Masterpieces of Suncook, New Hampshire, that advises users on how to care for their Japanese-made tools.

Probably the primary advantage of drawing a saw rather than pushing it is that the blade can be a lot thinner without any danger of buckling, and it can therefore make a much narrower cut. Users say Japanese saws make a different sound when they are cutting and that the feel is different. Some describe it as a surgical cut.

Besides the control factor that makes Japanese tools popular in the U.S., they are made of much better steel and hold a sharper cutting edge longer. The blades of some of them are made of the same kind of steel that is used in swords, which can be honed to the sharpness of a razor and will slice through some woods like a surgical knife going through a melon. (My colleague Steve Zimmerman, who does a lot of business with Japan, makes the interesting analogy that "pull" instead of "push" also applies to Japan's management philosophy.)

American craftsmen who use Japanese tools say that a well-sharpened plane cuts wood surfaces so smoothly that they take on a natural sheen that does not require sanding or finishing and gradually develops a rich, natural patina that adds to their appearance, feel, and spirit.

Japanese craftsmen sharpen their tools every workday and some tune them—a quality of care that is spreading among Japanized craftsmen in the U.S.

Handicrafts were commonplace in America until well into the 1900s, and many craftsmen achieved a standard of quality and beauty comparable to what was being produced in Japan. Unfortunately this tradition did not survive the industrial age. Now we have a turning back in America, a return to preindustrial handicraft occupations requiring the use of fine tools and years of developing skill and style, and there is much to be learned from contemporary Japan.

Because of the master-apprentice system that prevailed in Japan for over a thousand years, practically everything produced in the country—woodenware, ceramic ware, lacquerware, etc.—was a piece of handicraft art. Boys, often as young as seven or eight, were apprenticed to skilled craftsmen for 15, 20, or 30 years before they were allowed to go out on their own. These traditions also resulted in raising toolmaking to the level of an art. Both of these traditions have been diminished in Japan by industrialization, but they have not disappeared.

I predict that the trend toward the use of Japanese hand-tools by American craftsmen will continue to spiral upwards—along with some of the Japanese philosophy of believing that wood has its own spirit and treating tools with greater respect.

Pride

The Japanese take pride in their country, in themselves, and in their accomplishments. They work with a diligence and dedication that would put most Americans to shame. A sincere respect for order, authority, and education is also a highly honed characteristic of the Japanese.

One of the primary economic advantages of the Japanese is that employees work harder and longer hours than Americans. The Japanese Labor Ministry says that Japanese workers average 2,116 hours *more* each year than American workers. Only around 40 percent of the vacation time available to Japanese workers is actually used.

Journalist-author David Halberstam has described the Japanese as "immigrants," with all the ambition and dedication that has traditionally distinguished the new citizens of the United States. The Japanese, he says, are not escapees from an old world to a new one. They are escapees from a feudal life of near slavery to a new, urban life of virtually total freedom.

The Japanese certainly have something most Americans have lost—an unquenchable thirst to achieve, to better themselves through hard work, education, perseverance, sacrifice. But these goals are not merely materialistic; they are also spiritual. And they are intimately tied to the pursuit of beauty—the art of doing well as an end in itself.

Japanese workers are intensely proud of their ability, their expertise. The idea of doing less than their best is virtually unthinkable. Generally speaking, Japanese repairmen and service-men know their business and do a good job. It is almost unheard of for them to overcharge or try to take advantage of a customer in some other way. They take pride in doing good work and in maintaining "face." The Japanese pride themselves on being hospitable and unselfish. Their sense of face—of pride in themselves and in their country—provides extraordinary motivation and makes them intensely nationalistic.

In contrast, a frightening percentage of American workers have little or no pride in what they do or in themselves. They are not highly motivated to do their best for their employer and seldom, if ever, relate their own efforts or behavior to the health and welfare of the country. This is true even when they are well paid and living high.

CHAPTER VI

Advantages of Friendship

For the most part, Americans admire and like the Japanese they meet on both business and social levels. The overwhelming majority of Americans who visit Japan as tourists are so impressed with the few Japanese they meet that they have difficulty verbalizing the strength of their feelings. Our need to like people and our reaction to the Japanese on an individual basis has resulted in the development of an uncountable number of relationships that have benefited the Japanese and Japan economically and culturally, and has been a major factor in U.S.-Japan affairs.

I knew many American importers back in the 1950s who persevered in their attempts to buy from Japan, despite linguistic and other cultural barriers, simply because they admired and personally liked the Japanese. In this situation these Americans were not motivated totally by a desire to make money by buying cheap in Japan and selling higher in the U.S.

I cannot say that the Japanese like us as much as we like them, but indications are that they do—or at least they try to! Virtually all polls covering the likes and dislikes of the Japanese (and they are even more addicted to polling than we are) indicate that most Japanese rate Americans over most other foreign nationalities. But the Japanese cannot afford to be sentimental or personal in their relations with the United States. They must be practical and pragmatic. They must act with their own interests foremost because, unlike the U.S., with its huge land mass and vast supply of resources, the Japanese cannot afford to make mistakes. Even one mistake could be disastrous to Japan's economy if it should concern oil or some other vital commodity of which the Japanese have practically none.

At the same time, because the Japanese are totally aware that their economic welfare is intimately linked to that of the United States, they go out of their way to conduct their affairs with us on as friendly a basis as possible, regardless of their personal feelings.

No doubt, the primary reason Americans and Japanese are attracted to each other is that we are opposites in many ways. The Japanese are racially and culturally homogeneous. They live in a small, tightly knit, tribal type of community with a highly refined social system that molds them into almost identical cogs. Both their geographical freedom and their personal freedoms are limited and controlled. They are under deep, permanent obligations to their families, their schools, their employers, and to Japan.

Americans, on the other hand, have been conditioned by a vast expanse of land that historically seemed to go on forever. We are a mixture of both races and cultures, as well as a montage of races and cultures that exist side by side, sometimes rent by violence, but mostly in peace. We pay allegiance to nobody if for some reason we don't want to—including our own parents and especially our schools, our employers, and our country.

We hold that individual freedom of choice and action is the highest law and that independence is the handmaiden of this law. We put up with an unbelievable amount of violence, inefficiency, stupidity, and other human weaknesses in the name of personal freedom.

Most Americans who go to Japan are attracted to the efficiency, the cleanliness, the order, the energy, and the accomplishments of the Japanese. They admire the refined social graces of the Japanese and are charmed by the products of a culture that has had over 2,000 years in which to learn the essence of beauty and many other aspects of graceful living. They are impressed by the Japanese, who themselves are highly refined products of this culture.

When the Japanese come to America, it is something like a moth breaking out of a cocoon. They do not have to be *Japanese* all the time. The invisible steel threads that bind and obligate them while they are in Japan are loosened and can be totally discarded if they choose to do so. This freedom is a heady experience for young Japanese in particular, who often find it difficult or impossible to go back to being Japanese after four or five years in the U.S.

Thus, while Japanese and Americans are so different that they are often very uncomfortable in each other's presence, the attractions between them are so powerful that they persist in their relationships. This is not to say, however, that this relationship will be long-lasting. Because of the role the U.S. played in the treaty between Japan and Russia in 1905, at which time the U.S. pressured Japan to limit its demands on Russia, the United States was perceived by many Japanese as having committed an unfriendly and unforgivable act. Beginning in 1909, there was a series of books based on the premise that Japan and the U.S. would eventually go to war against each other. In less then five years, the U.S. and Japan went from being friends to being adversaries. It is not unthinkable that sometime in the future the "economic war" in which we are already engaged might lead to more serious conflict.

Swords *vs.* Hammers

The highly structured, minutely defined Japanese business system has been a major factor in the economic success of the country. At the same time, the unstructured, ill-defined system in the United States has always been one of our major strengths because it has given free rein to the imagination, abilities, and ambitions of mavericks in our society. Says M.I.T. professor David Birch, "We have a tradition of wild and crazy people. Japan doesn't have this tradition. We have an enormous comparative advantage."

(Birch is the man who first pointed out that most new jobs in the United States are created by small companies, not large ones, and that new ideas and the freedom to put them into action are one of our most important resources.)

Psychologically, though, the Japanese do have many advantages over Americans. For one thing, they think of themselves as "round," in the sense that they are conscious of things from a 360-degree viewpoint, while Americans tend to think of things and themselves as being made up of four sides—the front, two sides, and a back. Americans are primarily concerned about the front of things, including their own bodies, while the Japanese think in terms of the whole and feel that they are totally on display or exposed in all directions.

The Japanese also tend to think of themselves as "swords," which must be kept sharp, polished, and poised at all times to repel an attack from any direction. I do not think we have to worry about the Japanese influence on our psychological profile—we are more like hammers than swords.

Still, if we do not learn our lesson well, the Japanese will surpass us in many areas that count. Returning to Japan in 1984 for the first time in 30 years, veteran *U.S. News & World Report* journalist Joseph Fromm said that the Tokyo he had come to know during the Occupation years had ceased to exist; that in its place was a "prosperous and bustling metropolis of gleaming skyscrapers, modish shops, and smart restaurants. The sidewalks are crowded with businessmen in three-piece suits and young men and women sporting the latest New York fashions."

Fromm added that downtown Tokyo resembled New York's Madison Avenue multiplied 100 times over. He could have added that Tokyo has several dozen "downtowns," each one of them a fascinating complex of office buildings, shops, restaurants, cafes, cabarets, theaters, and bars. The same can be said for all of Japan. This does not mean, however, that Japan has been "Westernized." Many Americans automatically equate modernization with Westernization. They see the modern aspects of Japan and assume without thinking that the Japanese are "just like Americans," with perhaps a few minor differences. This assumption is the source of much of the misunderstanding that plagues our relations with Japan.

Most Japanese who are old enough to remember the war and the Occupation by American troops are still grateful to the U.S. They know only too well that it was the United States that freed them from a dictatorial, militaristic, still feudal government—that planted the seeds for democracy and made it possible for them to create this entirely new world for themselves and their children.

But this gratitude does not prevent them from being serious competitors and continuing to take advantage of our blind spots and weaknesses.

Becoming No. 1

However, we do not have to be concerned about Japan becoming No. 1 in the world unless we simply give up. The Japanese have the desire, but they do not have the means. There are just too many handicaps—physical, as well as psychological—that they cannot overcome.

Hideaki Kase, a political and economic commentator writing in the prestigious journal *Zaikai*, says indirectly that Japan is incapable of becoming the top economic power in the world because it is not a nation-state but a tribal society, requiring consensus before it can act in unison. This lack of flexibility, he adds, makes it difficult for the Japanese to handle crises with other nations. He goes on to say that under the umbrella of American protection and indulgence, the Japanese have become self-confident and arrogant and are unable to respond effectively to outside forces.

The world may be fortunate that Japan does have this vital weakness, a weakness that can be taken advantage of both directly and indirectly in meeting and competing with the Japanese. But, again, we have to be aware of the weakness and know how to take advantage of it while cleaning up our own act at the same time.

In the late 1950s and early 60s, it was often predicted that Japan would outstrip the United States economically in 20 or so years. On the surface, it appears that the country has succeeded on a per capita basis because there are fewer poor people in Japan than in the U.S. But many thoughtful Japanese do not accept the idea that Japan is No. 1 in the world or even that Japan is a world leader. They say Japan does not have the basic requisites for world leadership (military power, a solid economic base, a philosophy that is universal in its appeal and applicability, and a democratic form of government in which individual freedom is a reality).

These Japanese add that only the United States has all of the prerequisites for being No. 1 in the world, and all that Japan wants—all that Japan is capable of—is being "Assistant to No. 1."

This "official" Japanese attitude is strongly disputed by many Westerners who were born in Japan, have lived there all their lives, and are perfectly fluent in the language. They say: "Don't let the Japanese fool you! They *want* to be No. 1 in the world! They *need* to be No. 1! It is something they can't help! They cannot rest or feel at ease until they are No. 1 in everything they do—in *everything*! It is an obsession built into the culture."

The Dangers of Ignorance

It is frightening to consider how important Japan is to the United States today in contrast to how little the average American businessman and politician knows about the country, despite all the books, magazine articles, television shows, and preaching by frustrated authors and Old Japan-Hands.

Of course, it is one thing to know something about the Japanese intellectually, which you can do through reading good books; it is altogether different to know them from personal experience, from actually living in the country with them and absorbing—physically, psychologically, and spiritually—the myriad nuances of their language, their attitudes, and their habits.

American high schools and universities should be sending far larger numbers of their students to Japan for study. American business should send droves of young executives to special schools in Japan and to intern there in their branches or with Japanese companies.

The chief executive officers of American companies with the slightest interest in Japan should stand in line at the American Graduate School of International Management, in Glendale, Arizona, to snap up graduates from the school's Far Eastern Area studies department. There are other American schools that also have Japanese culture, language, and business courses, but their graduates also are usually unable to find jobs involving Japan.

Sometimes the American government (Congress and the President) seems to recognize that American ignorance of Japan is a serious political and economic handicap. In 1975, in one of these rare moments, Congress passed and the President signed legislation creating the Japan-United States Friendship Commission, which still is the only American government entity whose sole purpose is to improve the understanding and friendship between the U.S. and a single foreign country.

The charter of the Commission emphasizes the need to strengthen the foundation of friendship and cooperation between the U.S. and Japan through educational and cultural exchange programs at the people-to-people level.

The Commission noted that the problems confronting the agency were formidable, since few Americans had more than a casual interest in Japan, and the language barrier was often seen as insurmountable—not to mention the other cultural barriers.

In any event, the Commission takes the long-range view that its limited efforts will contribute to the gradual development of a broader base of knowledge about Japan among Americans and that future problems on the national level could be resolved in an atmosphere of mutual understanding and respect. Funding for the Commission comes from part of the Japanese government repayments for U.S. facilities built in Okinawa and later turned over to Japan and from other postwar American assistance to Japan.

Positive Programs

In 1982, Youth for Understanding, one of the two largest youth exchange organizations authorized by the Department of State, inaugurated a Special Japan-U.S. Exchange Program under which 100 senior high school students are sent to Japan each summer for two months of living with Japanese families. The Japanese government pays for the students' transportation.

In 1984, the U.S. began an annual program of inviting 47 Japanese senior high school students (one from each prefecture) to spend a year in the United States as another way of promoting mutual understanding between the two nations.

In 1985, the Rockefeller Foundation launched a three-year, $1.5 million fellowship program to encourage the teaching of foreign languages in the U.S. Each year, 100 outstanding language instructors are selected to receive a grant of $4,500 to spend their summers in the country whose language they teach. The fellowships are administered by a cooperative of language teachers.

While positive, all of these programs are mere gestures in the right direction. Large-scale, wholesale programs are needed to even begin to bridge the cultural chasm that separates Japan and the United States.

One important obstacle to bridge building is the very strong feeling among some Japanese that the U.S. has let them and the rest of the world down by not exercising its role as the leader of the free world more effectively. Besides expecting the U.S. to follow a sound macroeconomic policy, which specifically includes taking into consideration the consequences its policies have on other countries of the world, Japan expects the U.S. to play a leading role in maintaining and reforming international economic institutions.

This obligation includes strengthening the free-trade system in regard to traditional goods, as well as working out fair and equitable adjustments of existing institutions to cope with the decline of some industries and the emergence of new highly technological industries.

Since the United States and Japan together account for nearly one-third of the world's GNP, Japan feels that both are obligated to help build a freer and more open international economic system that will allow all countries to benefit and develop to the maximum. Of course, the two countries do not see their own roles and responsibilities in this area in the same way, and until they can effectively reduce their differences they will be faced with conflicts of interest that continue to undermine their relations.

THE INTERNATIONAL VIEW

Another Japanese characteristic I admire— and which I believe we should emulate more energetically—is their international orientation. This is not a pure and certainly not a totally positive characteristic, however. As in so many other areas of their life, the Japanese have two perspectives when it comes to their view of themselves and the outside world.

On one hand, the Japanese are conspicuously provincial, often to the point of xenophobia. At the same time, they tend to take a global approach in their business. As the Japanese say so often, they have no choice. With a tiny land base, a huge population, and few natural resources, the Japanese economy could not have progressed far beyond the cottage-industry level without a substantial import/export program.

This imperative is drummed into the Japanese as they grow up—as part of the educational process, as well as part of their learning how to be Japanese. This educational and cultural conditioning is, of course, responsible for Japan's being a nation of exporters, which in turn is the foundation for the country's extraordinary economic success.

In contrast, most American businessmen are not only provincial, a significant percentage of them are abysmally ignorant of the rest of the world. What is worse, many of them couldn't care less.

The reasons for our cultural and economic myopia are obvious enough—a huge country, an enormous amount of natural resources, a vast consumer market, and an educational and political system that either ignores or gives short shrift to the world at large.

Many of the ills that plague the United States today are a direct result of our ignorance of the world beyond our shores and borders. Our government and business leaders continue to ignore the importance of language and culture in dealing with foreign nations. Because they do not appreciate the importance of these realities, they generally do not even use the experts who are available. The ongoing results of this intellectual failure range from major business mishaps to stupid, destructive wars.

The United States would benefit enormously, as would our allies and trading partners, if we officially incorporated the concept of internationalism into our educational system, made it mandatory that our State Department officials and personnel speak the language and be intimately familiar with the culture of the country they are assigned to, and encouraged more American manufacturers of all sizes to develop export programs.

Americans tend to think of Japan in terms of huge companies and large, Zaibatsu-type conglomerates, and these are indeed prominent. But Japan's impressive "economic miracle" of the past few decades was primarily accomplished by thousands of small manufacturers and exporters. In fact, hundreds of Japan's most famous companies, from Sony to Canon, were very small organizations in the 1950's and raised the Japanese economy up as they grew.

The American market is no longer able to indiscriminately absorb the products of the rest of the world without having a balancing export program. It is therefore essential that we do some of the things that the Japanese have done—that all Americans be made aware of how foreign trade works and how it benefits people and nations when it is done properly.

The challenge is intellectual and therefore educational, and until it is addressed on a national basis as a vital concern, the response to the challenge will be piecemeal and inadequate. Again, we can look at Japan as an example that vividly demonstrates the opportunities presented by looking at the world as one huge marketplace that should be open to all.

The Importance of Language

Fewer than half of all colleges and universities in the U.S. require foreign language study for a bachelor's degree, down from 90 percent in 1966. Only around one-quarter of all American institutions of higher learning require students to study European or American history or literature. Only 14 percent of them require courses in the civilizations of classical Greece and Rome. The result of this, says the National Endowment for the Humanities, is that most American students are deprived of any sense of a common culture or heritage from the past.

Among the most obvious lessons the United States should learn from Japan is the importance of foreign languages in commerce, international relations, and cultural exchanges. All Japanese students are required to study a foreign language for eight years. Most of them study English. Most of them do not learn to speak English—or even read or write it well—but all of them are exposed to it, and hundreds of thousands of them go on to study English for several additional years.

The reason why more Japanese do not become fairly proficient in English is that their teachers are seldom fluent in spoken English, the emphasis is on reading, and few of the students have sufficient opportunities to practice with native English speakers.

Many students who pursue the study of English on their own go to special private schools where they are tutored by foreign teachers in small classes. Many of the "Japan 500" companies employ from one to two or three dozen foreigners to teach English to their employees. Employees of all ages and in all levels of management attend these classes, often including presidents and directors who are in their 60s and 70s.

One 78-year-old president of a major corporation summed it up nicely. "Over half of my business is with English-speaking foreigners. It is impossible to have a good working relationship with someone if you cannot talk to them directly, heart to heart."

The heroic efforts of the Japanese to learn foreign languages has been one of the major factors in their economic success since 1952.

The American military forces were smart enough during the Pacific war (1941–1945) to send several hundred young Americans to Japanese language training schools in preparation for the Occupation of Japan. They should have sent several thousand to the schools, because a significant percentage of these men have since made important contributions to Japanese-American relations, and one can only imagine how much the United States could have benefited if there had been thousands instead of hundreds.

I read somewhere that when we got involved in the Vietnam war, there was not one American-born Vietnam linguist or specialist in the State Department. This source estimated that if there had been ten Vietnamese-speaking Americans who were intimately familiar with the country available to the Pentagon and the State Department, it could have saved 50,000 lives and hundreds of billions of dollars.

Most American businessmen (and diplomats) have yet to learn this lesson, despite the horrendous problems and the loss of billions of dollars in business and despite personal frustrations at not being able to communicate with their counterparts in Japan, except through Japanese interpreters.

The United States loses a lot of face because of this failing, which is regularly brought to the attention of the Japanese public by the news media and just as often related to the Ugly American syndrome. Such commentators as Fuji Kamiya, a professor of international relations at Keio University in Tokyo, point out that all of the staff of the Japanese Embassy in Washington, D.C., speak English, while only a few Americans assigned to the U.S. Embassy in Tokyo speak Japanese. Kamiya adds that the U.S. State Department is just as remiss in briefing the President about proper etiquette during his visits to Japan and meetings with the Japanese prime minister.

Our problem is a combination of provincial ignorance, cultural arrogance, and stupidity on the part of our government and educational leaders. The examples are endless. General Motors reportedly tried to sell its Nova cars in Latin America. In Spanish, *Nova* means "It won't go." Parker Pen is said to have run a Spanish-language ad in Latin America that indicated their new pen had contraceptive benefits. Spanish is a very simple language compared to Japanese, so you can imagine some of the mistakes that have been made in Japan.

It is funny, yes. But it is also tragic.

The typical American businessman—and the higher they are, the better the example—simply refuses to believe that the Japanese language constitutes a barrier. "Hell!" he says, "you can hire an interpreter for a few bucks! Anyway, most Japanese speak English!"

It has been pointed out many times that fluency in a foreign language is more important to an American businessman in Japan than a diploma from Harvard Business School. In fact, very little of what goes into American business education is of any value in Japan. Some U.S. colleges of business administration are even teaching their students that it is a waste of time to develop personal relationships with customers because more and more business is being handled by computer.

That American government and business leaders remain unconcerned by this national weakness doesn't make sense even when explained by such stock phrases as cultural insensitivity and cultural arrogance. If experience is any guide, they are not likely to change their attitudes or behavior until a major financial crisis can be tied directly to their inability to communicate with their overseas markets.

Talking without Communicating

There is a profound difference in the essence of person-to-person communication in Japan and in the United States. The primary purpose of communicating in the U.S. is to convey information and understanding. The first purpose of communication in Japan is to convey moods and feelings.

Effective communication in the U.S. depends on the precise use of clear, concrete words. English is designed to be used in logical, cool sentences that convey specific meanings. Communication in Japan tends toward imprecise words and nonverbal signals. Japanese is designed to be used to create the proper social and emotional relationship between the people concerned.

This means that most Japanese-American conversations are never really on the same wavelength. The words of each are filtered through his or her own cultural prism and are changed in the process. This means, of course, that in order to begin to communicate with each other more effectively we must be aware of and sensitized to these differences.

Japan's Ministry of Posts and Telecommunications is now engaged in a long-term project to refine a telephone system that automatically translates Japanese into English and vice versa. The English-to-Japanese version of the system went on sale in June 1985 but is far from perfected. The mechanical translator at this point can only understand speakers whose voices and accents have been programmed into the system.

Once the bugs are out of the automatic translation system, it can be applied to conference and personal units, as well as telephones. This will be a fantastic advance in world affairs, in all aspects of life, but it will not solve the problems of cross-cultural communication. That will continue to require the human touch.

During the U.S. military Occupation of Japan from 1945 to 1952 and the following decade, Americans found many of the attempts of the Japanese to use English both irritating and humorous. This bastardization of English-Japanese was derisively referred to as "Japlish," a term coined by some unknown foreign writer who lived and worked in Japan long before World War II and the Occupation years. I don't remember where I picked up on the word, but I began using it in the early 1950s to describe the Japanized English that appeared in everything from advertisements and public signs to government-issued White Papers.

There were so many examples of Japlish during these years—and some of them were terribly funny—that some people collected them, and, for a while, one of the English-language newspapers in Tokyo ran a column featuring humorous Japlish signs.

One sign in Tokyo, for example, read: WOMEN FITTED IN THE UPPER STORY (over a brassiere shop). A sign near the Roppongi Intersection in Tokyo proclaimed, LET'S BE QUIET BY OURSELVES. A French restaurant proudly advertised its POISON! instead of its *poisson*. One of the favorites of Old Japan-Hand Michael C. Sodano: "Ladies dresses downstairs. Have fits upstairs."

But, while Americans and other English-speaking people in Japan were laughing, the Japanese were learning and their influence was spreading around the world like a tidal wave. I certainly don't believe we should ape Japlish signs, but what we are already doing is using English the way the Japanese are trained to use Japanese—speaking and writing in circumlocutions and euphemisms. In a society in which all behavior was severely prescribed and people had to be extremely cautious about offending anyone, it became customary for them to speak in the most general terms, to avoid direct statements and final commitments. The primary aim was to avoid incurring any responsibility.

We are hearing more and more of that kind of English in the U.S.—something we do not need to copy from the Japanese.

Intelligence

By all accounts, Japan has the largest, most sophisticated, and most effective worldwide economic intelligence-gathering network ever seen. The intelligence activities of either of Japan's two largest trading companies, Mitsui and Mitsubishi, surpass those of most countries—and rival those of the United States and Russia.

Japan's economic intelligence corps dates back to the 1870s, almost immediately after the fall of the feudal Tokugawa Shogunate and the restoration of the emperor to power. It was not until the late 1950s and 1960s, however, with the rapid rise of Japan's economy and the development of high-speed electronic communications, that the Japanese international economic news corps came into its own.

It is therefore all the more astounding to consider that several key segments of American industry still do not have intelligence-gathering offices in Japan and that it was not until 1984 that the U.S.'s electronics industry set up its first information-gathering service in Tokyo.

This belated "marketing maneuver" was opened in June 1984 by the American Electronics Association (AEA), which has some 2,500 corporate members, in cooperation with the U.S. Department of Commerce. The DOC agreed to pay half of the operating costs of the office for the first two years.

The purpose of the office is "to collect, analyze, and disseminate information about technical and political trends surrounding the Japanese electronics industry" and transmit the information to its members in the U.S. The American manager of the AEA's Tokyo office made a point that I and dozens of others have been harping on since the early 1960s—namely, that Japan has one of the largest and best trade presses in the world. But, because it is in Japanese, its content remains unknown to some 98 percent of all American businessmen who should be vitally interested in it.

This, again, is indicative of the attitude and behavior that has traditionally characterized American businessmen and the American government in their relations with Japan. While better late than never is still valid, it does not speak well for the acumen or foresight of American businessmen.

CHAPTER VII

Working Japanese Style

S azo Idemitsu, founder of Idemitsu Oil Company, the third largest oil company in Japan, was one of the most extraordinary men in a long line of extraordinary men in Japan's modern history. Born in 1885, Idemitsu founded the forerunner of Idemitsu Oil in 1911. He inherited the best spiritual values of feudal Japan: a total commitment to the ideals of peace and happiness achieved through selfless striving for the benefit of mankind.

Idemitsu's use of practical wisdom and his insistence on giving people precedence over systems and "knowledge" made him a popular figure even before World War I, but these values did not endear him to Japanese militarists. Looking back on a lifetime of extraordinary achievement, Idemitsu once said that his success was based primarily on unlearning conventional knowledge and concentrating on how to apply himself to the practice of working with people to achieve great goals.

He added: "We human beings have a tendency to become captives of what we have been taught as knowledge, as a result of which we often lose sight of the prime purpose of human beings, which is to live in peace and friendship."

Throughout his long life, Idemitsu taught that every project, every problem should be approached with "man as its center." With man as the center, he said, there would be no conflict with any political or economic ideology, since Man transcends all other considerations.

In Idemitsu's view, Western cultures are based on knowledge as the fountainhead of all things, while Japanese culture is based on the concept that the heart—human feelings—is paramount in all things. The Western way leads to conflict and struggle; the Japanese way, to peace and harmony, said Idemitsu.

Idemitsu also taught that luxury was deadly to human beings. He was one of Japan's leading advocates of the *Seiren Keppaku*, or "Clean Poverty," principle—a concept that was a major factor in the Japanese philosophy of life down to modern times. The controversial entrepreneur also said American companies tend to be operated in a logical, reasoned, and rigid way. This, he said, creates friction and conflict, since people do not think or behave in such a manner.

When the Japanese use the word "responsibility," it has both a moral and spiritual connotation and goes beyond the legal sense, which is one of the reasons why they traditionally did not use written contracts in business arrangements. Idemitsu taught that a salary should not be the price of a person's labor, but a guarantee of the employee's livelihood. During hard times, he did not fire anyone. All shared whatever was available. He kept apologizing for the hardships imposed on the workers. Their reply: "Let's not talk about money and get on with the work."

Idemitsu did not pay for overtime work. His employees would not accept it. When he announced that he would abide by the new postwar labor standards law and pay overtime, his employees refused to take the additional money. When they had work they could not finish by quitting time, they took it home and did it there. They told him, "We work to get the work done, not to make extra money."

Idemitsu reminded everyone that prior to the fall of the Tokugawa Shogunate in 1868, only merchants worked strictly for money. Virtually everyone else in the country worked for a guaranteed livelihood detached from the idea of income. The idea of selling one's labor for a specific amount of money was alien to the Japanese.

Employees of American companies work for their own private benefit. In Japan employees work for their own benefit, as well as the benefit of their co-workers, the company, and the country.

We have long known in the West that the ultimate wealth is a sense of contentment with what one has—a wealth of the spirit and mind rather than physical wealth. We need to revive and teach this in our schools.

Idemitsu's idea of morality is expressed in the terms *Gojoh-Gojo*—"Mutual Concession, Mutual Help." To him, a peaceful and happy life is all there is to religion and philosophy.

Amtrak is a perfect example of some of the differences in the character and motivations of Americans and Japanese. For most of its history, Amtrak has not been successful. Japan's *Shinkan Sen*, popularly known in English as the "Bullet Train," was inaugurated in 1964 and is still a marvel of technology and human efficiency. There has never been a fatal accident to a paying passenger in its operation.

The Bullet Trains are clean and in good shape, and they maintain their schedules with clockwork precision. The trains leave Tokyo Central Station (at 12- to 18-minute intervals during peak hours) on the second. They cruise at 200 kilometers per hour. When the conductor announces that a stop will be for *two minutes*, the doors close and the trains leave in *120 seconds*!

How can Amtrak be so different—often inefficient, at times unsafe, so much of an embarrassment to the country? The answer may appear complex, but it is not. An organization is a direct reflection of the character and personality of the people who make it up. It would appear that many of the people who are involved with Amtrak, including management, employees, and the various government officials, are not sincere, not diligent, not concerned, not proud, not patriotic enough to do the job that should be done.

They do not regard themselves as personally responsible for the efficiency and safety of the Amtrak system. For the most part, they do no more than the minimum necessary not to get fired. When even 10 percent of the employees of a large, detailed operation like Amtrak do not perform at a high level of excellence, the overall performance drops dramatically.

Of course, most Amtrak employees want the organization to continue and succeed, but not necessarily because it is needed; not because it is or could be of vital importance to the nation; not out of any sense of embarrassment for themselves, the company, or the country, but because they don't want to lose their jobs.

Like Amtrak, the whole American economic, social, and political system suffers from malignancies that weaken the body and heart of the country. One of the most cancerous of these ills is the refusal of individuals to take personal responsibility—sometimes for anything!

Most of Amtrak's problems, most of the problems of the country, stem from weaknesses in the American people in areas where the Japanese are conspicuously strong. We do not have to copy Japanese ethics or morality to bring about a substantial improvement in the operating efficiency of Amtrak and other American enterprises. But we can certainly look at them and compare ourselves to them as a means of measuring how far we have fallen from grace and as an inspiration for rehabilitating our society.

MANAGEMENT PRINCIPLES

The adversary relationship between American companies and their employees is unthinkable in Japanese terms and points up how far we still have to go in the Japanization of American business. Just one example that occurred recently in Iwai City, Japan, graphically demonstrates the fundamental differences between our two systems. Shuji Sakuma, the president of a successful engineering company, proposed giving all his employees a month's paid vacation every year during the slack season, when the plant normally operated at half capacity.

Just imagine this offer being made to American employees! To a man and woman, they would jump up and down with joy, accept the offer without a second thought and do their best to enjoy themselves at their employer's expense.

Not the Japanese! The key engineers and salesmen in the company, totally shocked that the president would even think of such a thing, formed a delegation to register a protest with the president and accused him of being insincere—which in the Japanese context is about as bad as you can get. The workers told the president that giving all of them so many days off would be bad for their morale because it would give all of them the impression that the company was not serious about its obligations to its customers or its employees.

Finally, the president and the employees worked out a compromise that the staff accepted only grudgingly—a few staggered days off during the year, with pay.

This attitude is not unusual in Japan. Hundreds of thousands—managers in particular—decline to take their annual holidays. IBM (Japan) distributes leaflets and posters pleading with its employees not to be ashamed to take their full vacations. One major biscuit manufacturer offers its employees special bonuses to encourage them to take all of their days off.

There is one school of thought in Japan that many workers do not take all their vacation time off because their houses and apartments are too small to be enjoyed during leisure time, they generally do not have gardens or yards that need any care their wives can't handle, few of them know or associate with their neighbors, their friends all work so they would not have anybody to buddy-around with, and so on.

This may be partly true, but it certainly does not explain a typical Japanese attitude that contrasts so strongly with that of Americans. I happen to believe that all of us, Japanese and Americans, work too hard too many days of the year. I believe that once living standards reach a certain comfortable level we should limit ourselves to four or even three days of work a week.

In the meantime, the American educational system should incorporate the Japanese concept that the relationship between employers and employees is a symbiotic one, that each is totally dependent on the other, and that there are fundamental mutual obligations that should govern the relationship and go beyond money considerations.

The Japanese discovered a long time ago that instruction in morality is an essential ingredient in the training of a future craftsman or journeyman worker, just as it is in the education of anyone for responsible citizenship. We have yet to learn this lesson, and once again we can look to Japan as a model.

Cutting Off Your Nose

The traditional relationship between American management and labor unions, one in which the two sides have faced each other as adversaries, is a prime example of the failure of the American system. For two vital segments of society that are totally dependent upon each other to behave like enemies goes beyond stupidity. It is a type of insanity.

The problem is primarily one of lack of knowledge about economics, coupled with a debilitating case of shortsightedness. A significant percentage of the labor leaders and workers of America are not wise enough to understand the results of their actions—which goes back to a failure in American education.

Here again, the partial Japanization of American unions would be a great step forward for union members, their employers, and the country. Employees who want a union should have their own independent "company" union, as the Japanese do. It might or might not be associated with a national federation. The company and union should maintain a team of delegates that meet regularly—at least once a week—to discuss any problems or concerns of either the employer or the staff and to reach mutually agreeable decisions on what to do about them.

These company and union delegates should be rotated on a regular basis, with no one holding the position of delegate for more than one year. The union delegates would remain full employees of the company and draw no salary and no benefits from any union fund. At least one management delegate should be on an executive vice president level, and in smaller companies the chief executive officer should sit in on the weekly meetings on a regular basis. Decisions arrived at by the delegates should be binding on both management and the union.

In this approach, both management and workers would tend to select the best possible delegates to represent their interests. The motivation would not be to outdo the other side, but to come to agreements that all could willingly accept and keep; that would benefit both labor and management—not to mention the people at large and the country.

For the past several years in Japan, the average Japanese worker has lost only fifteen minutes and fifty seconds of work time per year because of strikes. In the U.S. during the same period, the average American worker lost three hours.

Democratizing the Workplace

Only about one-fourth of the several hundred Japanese-owned manufacturing facilities in the United States have unions, and most of these are in seafood processing plants in Alaska. Generally speaking, most Japanese plants in the U.S. are not unionized because the relationship between management and employees is friendly, trusting, and cooperative. Instead of management and labor being in opposing camps, regularly snarling at each other and fighting, workers and managers in most Japanese plants in America regard themselves as being on the same team and work together.

There is far less physical separation of management and labor in Japanese-run companies. Japanese managers generally do not isolate themselves in private offices, maintain their own exclusive dining rooms, or have their own private parking spaces. In many companies, the managers wear the same uniforms as the workers.

According to American employees of many Japanese companies, the whole atmosphere is different. Instead of distrust, ill will, arguments, and fights, which are commonplace in many American factories, there is trust and goodwill and a total absence of verbal and physical violence.

In typical Japanese-owned plants, individual workers are taught to do several jobs, including repairing equipment that breaks down. They don't have to stand around and wait for an "approved union man" to come and do something that they can do themselves. This increases motivation and makes the workers more flexible. The result is that both quality and production tend to be higher in Japanese-managed companies.

Certainly, not all Japanese managers stationed in the U.S. are competent by any standards, and some of them are not easy to work for. They sometimes cannot communicate well with their American employees and are often criticized for not advancing American employees to higher managerial positions. But on the average their reputation is good.

The general attitude of Japanese management in the U.S. is, if you treat people right, with fairness and respect, there is no need for a union, regardless of the industry. As for the quality of American workers themselves, the consensus of Japanese opinion seems to be that there is a much greater range of ability among American workers than among Japanese workers. Most Japanese workers are described as having about the same level of competence. In America, on the other hand, there are large numbers of workers with superior ability, as well as significant numbers with inferior ability, according to Japanese measurements.

Despite the growing competitive power of Japanese automakers in the U.S., some industry leaders see the Japanese as providing them with an opportunity to break the stranglehold the unions have had on the industry in the past.

The GM/Toyota joint venture in Fremont, California, is, again, indicative of the quality and degree of Japanese influence in American business. The new company went out of its way to eliminate the petty social differences between blue and white collars that have angered production workers in the past, noted *New York Times News Service* writer John Holusha.

Holusha added: "Everybody, including Toyoda (the top Toyota man in the factory), eats in the same cafeteria, and preferred parking places no longer exist. Ping-Pong tables, basketball hoops, and volleyball nets have been installed in empty sections of the cavernous plant for use during lunch time. Employees are being offered their own business cards, to emphasize the importance of each individual."

The United Automobile Workers union members working at the ex-GM plant had a very bad reputation, involving allegations of rampant drug abuse and poor discipline. Now the workers are divided into quality-circle type teams of 5 to 12 people under a "leader." Each member of the team is expected to be able to do the work of each of the other members—exactly the way similar teams operate in Japan.

When GM operated the plant, the UAW had dozens of job classifications, with absolutely no crossing over. Now there is one classification for ordinary workers and three for skilled technicians.

In the meantime, some American unions that have not yet understood the error of their ways are coming up with new tactics in their battle with management—ranging from public relations-type approaches to getting companies involved in expensive court battles in an attempt to force them to agree to the union's demands. They continue to ignore the lessons to be learned from Japan.

The Japanese learn quickly. They are much more careful now in hiring American workers for their U.S. operations. Just as in Japan, employees are screened rigorously to make sure that those who do not have the "right attitude" are eliminated.

Those who are selected are then thoroughly and continuously indoctrinated in the Japanese way of doing things. For people who are going to be in charge of quality control and other key operations, this often means several weeks of intensive on-the-job training in Japan.

One of the best examples of an American company operation that has been deliberately and successfully Japanized is the Cadillac engine plant of General Motors in Livonia, Michigan. Beginning in 1980, Robert Strammy, the plant manager, and two of his assistants began restructuring the management and operation of the plant from top to bottom—a process that has been minutely detailed in a book, *Transforming the Workplace*, by three men who carried out the reformation.

In brief, layers of management were eliminated, the gulf between supervisors and workers was reduced, union leaders were weaned away from the "we against them" syndrome, workers were divided into "business teams" of 8 to 15 people and given significant autonomy, union-designed job designations were eliminated, all workers were trained to do several jobs, workers were regularly rotated to other jobs and to other teams, and technical experts were taught to assist rather than dictate to workers.

The Japanization process went further. Reserved parking for managers and executives' dining rooms were eliminated. Managers began dressing like other employees. Weekly meetings of all business teams and general meetings of all employees were instituted, and employees were encouraged to get involved in improving the looks and ambience of the workplace.

The transformation process took three years. By 1985, production cost at the plant was down 50 percent, productivity was up 100 percent, and absenteeism had plummeted to less than half of what it had been before the change.

The Healthy Worker

The employees of many larger Japanese factories and sales companies start each day with a *Chorei shiki*, or Morning Ceremony. Other companies hold *chorei* every other morning or in some cases just once a week. When I joined the Japan Travel Bureau (JTB) in Tokyo in 1953, I was surprised at this daily practice. The manager of the department would make various announcements and then give a brief pep talk. If nothing else, this little ceremony reminded us that we were members of a specific group within JTB and that the reputation and standing of the department—and, by extension, JTB's position in the travel industry—depended on how well we performed our duties.

The *chorei* in other Japanese companies range from equally brief meetings to enthusiastic rallies at which the employees sing the company song and charge up their psychic batteries by shouting slogans. The *chorei* are used by company management to announce new policies or projects and brief employees about the current situation. Employees are encouraged to ask questions and make suggestions. (The presidents of smaller, old-family companies often use the *chorei* to make boring speeches.)

Some employees meet early and take group calisthenics as a way of building better health, as well as team spirit.

There is obviously some merit in the *chorei*. Some American companies have a long history of Monday morning meetings for managers. I suggest that all American companies look seriously at the idea of having all employees meet briefly every morning! Of course, care would have to be taken that these meetings do not end up being "bitch" sessions—something that American employees are very good at.

Major American corporations have historically provided various kinds of recreational facilities or opportunities for their ranking executives. But it was not until the Japanese influence began making itself felt throughout the American economy that these corporate executives began thinking about the health and welfare of their workers.

While few, if any, American companies have gone as far as to conduct early morning group calisthenics for their employees, require the singing of company pep songs, or send their employees to behavior modification boot camps, as many Japanese companies do, a growing number now have fully integrated physical fitness and recreational programs for their employees, which in effect accomplish some of the same aims as group recreational and motivational activities in companies in Japan.

Sentry Insurance Company of Scottsdale, Arizona, is one good example of the blending of Japanese and American concepts in corporate health and productivity. Sentry maintains its own physical fitness club on the corporate premises, including a workout gym, jogging trails, treadmills, rowing machines, a swimming pool, and courts for basketball, racquetball, and tennis. The locker room is equipped with showers and such amenities as shampoo, hair dryers, shorts and socks, and T-shirts imprinted with the company's insignia. Sentry's director of human resources says the physical fitness program results in fewer illnesses among employees, reduces absenteeism, and increases productivity.

Sentry also provides its employees with personal counseling, stress-related testing, a stop-smoking program, a weight-reduction program, a full-time nurse, and a "quiet room" for relaxation, meditation, or prayer. The fitness center is open daily from 10:00 A.M. to 6:30 P.M. and on Saturdays from noon to 5:00 P.M. to all employees, their families, and retirees.

Other companies in Arizona that have similar recreational and health-enhancing programs for their employees include Honeywell Inc., Sperry Aerospace & Marine Group, Motorola Inc., Mountain Bell, First Interstate Bank, the Salt River Project, and KNIX Radio. The facilities and programs vary, but all are aimed at improving both the mental and physical health of employees and thereby both their morale and productivity. At Honeywell, where employees often have hectic schedules requiring that they come in early and work late, the company gives them time off to run or take other forms of exercise during working hours.

LEARNING FROM THE JAPANESE

Japan buys over 15 percent of all U.S. agriculture exports. One out of every 20 acres in the U.S. is cultivated for exports to Japan. Japan is the biggest buyer of American wheat, corn, soybeans, cotton, tobacco, citrus fruit, pork, and beef. Looked at from the Japanese side, the U.S. supplies over 40 percent of all Japan's farm imports. Japan's second largest supplier of farm produce, Australia, provides only 10 percent of its total farm imports.

These statistics indicate that having just "learned" a few lessons from the Japanese, it is far too early for us to rest on our laurels. Japanese corporate managers do not aim for quick profit. They aim for market share! Getting and keeping a significant share of the market is far more important than short-term profits because only a share of the market guarantees that a company will stay in business. This is a lesson many American businessmen have not fully grasped.

Management Training

The Japanese approach to training managers is basically the opposite of the American way. They look for management candidates with broad educational backgrounds and then bring them up through the company ranks in many different departments. By the time they become general managers, they have had a wealth of experience in many different areas and are able to think and plan in a far more holistic way than their American counterparts can.

Japanese managers spend more of their time thinking and talking about ways to improve their products and their services than American businessmen do. It is estimated that Japanese managers spend 40 percent of their time discussing and debating new products, new ideas, and new ways of doing things better.

The Japanese notion of an ideal leader is someone who is broadminded, pays no attention to detail, and often does nothing except inspire people by his "image" of knowledge and power. Such men are often called *O-Mono*, or "Big Thing (Man)." They arc viewed as having an abundance of virtue and as deserving of the extraordinary power they yield without doing anything other than making their wishes known.

Larger Japanese companies do not hire entry-level employees for specific jobs, and white-collar workers in particular are moved from one department to another many times during their working careers. Thus neither work skills nor even fields of study are significant considerations in the hiring procedure. The important thing is that the employees learn the company philosophy and how to cooperate and act in the best interest of the company.

Part of the training that new employees go through in Japan is "spiritual training." Some of this training at Nissho Iwai, the giant trading company, consists of a four-day retreat in a company facility outside of Tokyo, where the new employees practice Zen meditation, during which they reflect on the meaning of corporate life, attend lectures on acting as a responsible member of society, and make speeches that are reviewed by their peers.

Another difference between American and Japanese business management: There is no "boss" in the American sense in most larger Japanese companies. There are only people who are senior in rank.

American businessmen have traditionally tended to regard their enterprises as totally independent entities—not human and not responsible to humanity. Their employees were treated more or less like bodies needed to fill slots and to do a certain amount of work. Many American companies continue to treat their workers as pieces of equipment and make little or no effort to encourage the development of pride or loyalty.

Until more American businessmen understand and accept the Japanese concept of an enterprise as a group of people whose highest priority is to serve the best interests of their customers, they will continue to find themselves in an adversary relationship with their own employees, with the government, and with the marketplace.

Bureaucracy

Japan's age of bureaucracy began in 1192, with the appearance of the Shogunate form of government, and came of age during the early decades of the Tokugawa Shogunate, which began in 1603. By 1640, there was hardly an area of life in Japan that was not integrated into a bureaucratic web that sought to control the social, as well as the economic and political, activity of the people.

This system was so detailed and so limiting that it virtually precluded original thought and made change nearly impossible. The effect that it had on the minds of the Japanese was profound. As their way of life became hidebound and homogenized, so did their minds. As their psychology changed to fit the patterns of life prescribed by the Shogunate bureaucracy, so did their language.

The United States is now entering its age of bureaucracy, and because we have seen what it did to Japan (and to China), we know what it is going to do to the United States, unless the trend is reversed. The bureaucratic system first forces a change in behavior—everything becomes minutely defined, standardized, and then regulated. This behavioral modification results in a subtle psychological change that gradually stultifies the mind. Finally, the language changes to fit the bureaucratic personality.

The mind of the bureaucrat loses its elasticity and spontaneity. It moves slowly and lethargically along prescribed paths. Any time the movement is disturbed, it has to start over again at the beginning. Intellectual capacity dries up. The bureaucratic mind looks at all outsiders as enemies. The language of the bureaucrat loses its concrete, specific form and becomes vague and often meaningless. Form becomes more important than substance. Rigid ceremony replaces reality.

Federal, state, and municipal governments are not the only black holes of bureaucratism in the United States. Most of our businesses and schools also suffer from bureaucratic hardening of the arteries and are operated in ways that are destructive to themselves, as well as to the people they pretend to serve.

Former businessman Reginald G. Damarell, who became a professor of education at the University of Massachusetts in 1970, says in *Education's Smoking Gun: How Teachers' Colleges Have Destroyed Education in America* that bureaucratization in education has resulted in the hiring of teachers with abysmal academic records; a widespread attitude that reading, writing, and math do not come first in education; and a lack of a "body of knowledge" in the educational curriculum. Damarell concludes that the American educational system has been damaged so badly by the bureaucratic approach that we are going to have a permanent "educational underclass" in this country.

The Japanese, who are masters at the art of bureaucracy, have been able to surmount some of its most serious handicaps by grafting on various techniques from outside the bureaucratic maze for communicating and dealing with emergencies. Their homogenized culture, along with their group-think, group-act approach to virtually all problems and projects, gives them an advantage Americans do not have. They have learned how to make bureaucratization work for them to a substantial degree.

With far less experience in the subtleties and intricacies of bureaucratism, Americans at this point are less capable of working effectively within its rigid structure. If we do not become more aware of what is happening and take specific steps to change our direction, our whole system will continue marching lockstep into bureaucratic muck that will drag us down as if we were obsolete dinosaurs.

Perhaps the primary advantage the Japanese bureaucracy has over its American counterpart is that only the best and brightest of its young men are allowed to become higher level bureaucrats. Once the candidates have been selected in a careful process of elimination, they are just as carefully educated and trained to fulfill the role of the professional bureaucrat. Only the very best rise to the top of the pyramid after years of experience in the key departments of their ministries.

In the U.S., on the other hand, it is often just the opposite. Those who are less qualified tend to go into government services, first for job security and second because they know they will not be expected to demonstrate any significant intelligence or ability.

Adopting the Japanese system of government bureaucracy outright is not a solution, but establishing a system that would make it impossible for any but the best and the brightest to rise to the top of the bureaucratic heap would be a place to start.

Competition

The Japanese are also driven by a competitive impulse that is unbounded and unending. Once they are out of school, however, the Japanese almost always express this competitiveness on a group basis: department against department within companies and company against company on the outside.

The primary motivation for group, rather than personal, competition in Japan is that in their hierarchically structured business system the Japanese cannot rise individually on the basis of merit and accomplishment. They must perform within the context of their group and advance as a group. Once they join one of the larger companies, this competitive spirit is directed outward toward other departments in their own company and toward other companies in the same field.

In the U.S., competition differs radically. Americans rise and fall on the basis of individual merit and performance, or at least on what is perceived as talent and achievement.

This means that many employees have no particular loyalty to a group within a company or to a company. We are conditioned to look out for No. 1. Nothing pleases an American more than to be promoted faster and higher than his peers. And many American executives feel no special loyalty or obligation to their companies. Offer them a better deal, and they will go from one company to another with the greatest of ease. The American system works well for talented individuals but it works against the cohesion, sustained interest, and energy that is essential for outstanding group and company effort.

We need to emphasize more strongly the concept and practice of cooperation and teamwork in our educational system—not necessarily to the point demanded by the Japanese, but certainly strongly enough to significantly improve the efficiency of our enterprises.

CHAPTER VIII

Competing Japanese Style

L ong before the advent of World War II, the Japanese were being lectured on the morality and righteousness of free trade by countries that paid homage to the principle but not the practice. As early as 1929, the warning went out from the British Embassy in Tokyo that Japan had already become a serious competitor in foreign trade and that its home market was being ignored by most Western nations.

In fact, decades before this, the British Embassy had informed its government that in many areas Japanese-made products were on a par with those made in England and were already competing with them in many markets of the world. Nobody in England—or the U.S.—paid any attention to this vital information.

Already by this time, the Japanese were being spurred on by the slogan "Japanese Spirit; Western Technology" *(Wa-Kon; Yo-Sai)*—a slogan most Westerners never heard of, ignored, or smiled at condescendingly. But, as so often happens, the students were to surpass the teachers, and it would soon be their turn to smile.

Of course, most Americans today feel that the Japanese took advantage of the U.S. consumer market to enrich themselves at our expense, while they maintained various barriers that pre-vented U.S. companies from doing business in Japan. There is no doubt that the Japanese exploited the great American market. There is also no doubt that many American businessmen were unable to get into the Japanese market during the 1960s and 1970s because of official and unofficial government barriers.

But there is another important reason why so many American companies either failed to get into Japan or failed after they got in: They were unable to understand and adapt to the Japanese way of managing a business. Their attitude was, if it works in the U.S., it will work in Japan. Most American managers assigned to branch offices or subsidiary companies in Japan soon learned, however, that the only viable approach to doing business there was a combination of Japanese and American methods. But, more often than not, their recommendations were ignored by their home offices.

PRODUCING

Capitalism has proven to be the most effective of all economic systems simply because self-interest is one of the strongest of all motivations. The biggest failing of capitalism is that money tends to take precedence over human-oriented morality. In the United States, self-interest, primarily manifested by the pursuit of financial profit, is the overriding morality. We measure virtually everything in terms of dollar cost and profit.

The bulk of the wealth of the United States, its resources and industrial capacity, is controlled (not owned, but *controlled*) by corporate executives whose primary function and aim is to create a profit, often by getting people to consume things they do not need. The foundations of the economy are therefore on very weak ground.

Ralph Nader, the consumer advocate, says the primary motivation of megabusiness in the United States is avarice and that the main driving force of the economy is greed, not need. He adds that American business is far more adept at creating wants than at fulfilling needs. He also accuses American business of being on government welfare and no longer able to recognize a truly free market.

Nader notes that Americans are being subjected to an enormous brainwashing campaign by megabusinesses to believe whatever they hear, to trust business to do what is right, never to challenge businessmen, to obey, not to think, to spend instead of save—exactly the opposite of what they should be doing if this country is to compete effectively with Japan and the rest of the world.

Nader also predicts that the housing industry in the U.S. will not really start taking advantage of new technology and moving ahead until the Japanese start importing prefab houses into the country.

A recent controversy over "Dial-a-porn" services offered by telephone is indicative of the money-morality that pervades American culture. In Phoenix, Arizona, executives of Mountain Bell readily admitted that they were aware of the controversial history of sexually explicit telephone services and chose to make their "Scoopline" available to such services for the extra income they knew it would generate. Mountain Bell dropped the sexual message services only after receiving a barrage of protest letters from parents of children dialing the well-publicized "porn" numbers and also being threatened by a lawsuit by a Maricopa County attorney.

The Japanese have not yet totally succumbed to the seductions of money as morality. Traditional Japanese culture was founded on the concept of frugality, sharing, and avoidance of the corrupting influence of the single-minded pursuit of profit.

Throughout Japan's long feudal age (1192–1868), the Japanese were taught that profit making was immoral. The elite Samurai class was expected not to engage in any money-making activity. Merchants, the traditional money makers, were on the bottom of the social scale, below craftsmen and farmers.

This teaching was institutionalized in the concept of *Seiren Keppaku*, or "Clean Poverty," which held that it is immoral and antisocial to accumulate more material goods than one needs for subsistence and that there is honor in getting by with as little as possible. The philosophy has been considerably diluted in recent decades, but it is still an important factor in the Japanese approach to business. Profit making is secondary in the context of Japanese business. The primary concern of a Japanese businessman is to develop a company that will grow and last, that will provide permanent jobs for his employees and himself, and to make a contribution to the welfare of the country!

In contrast, the primary concern of most American businessmen is profit—to make as much money as possible within the shortest possible time. This single variation in the morality of Japanese and Americans makes all the difference in the world in the way we go about managing and operating our businesses.

In his book *Trade War: Greed, Power and Industrial Policy on Opposite Sides of the Pacific*, Steven Schlosstein put it this way: "Japanese companies are in the business of making products, whereas American companies are in the business of making money." Not totally true, of course, but true enough to emphasize the point.

Until we become wise enough and culturally mature enough to understand that a company is a social enterprise with fundamental responsibilities to society—that it is not just the private property of an individual or a bunch of absentee stockholders to operate for their benefit—we will be morally off base, as well as at a serious disadvantage in competing with Japan.

I am not suggesting government ownership or any other form of socialism or communism. What I am proposing is that American businessmen try to understand that they and their companies will benefit more in the long run if they change both their philosophy and operating procedures to be more in line with the Japanese system of integration with society.

A wonderfully inspiring example of one American's fight against money morality was reported in a recent edition of *Inc.* magazine. Jerry Juliano, the proprietor of a restaurant in Warrendale, Pa., decided to eliminate all prices from his menus and accept whatever his customers wanted to pay for the meals they ate. He took the action, he said, because he wanted to show that business could be done on the basis of trust.

As soon as word of Juliano's new system got out, patronage soared—and his monthly revenues increased 25 percent. Most of his old, as well as new, customers voluntarily paid about the same prices that had previously appeared on the menus. At the time of the story, only two customers had walked out without paying anything.

One of Juliano's customers was a meat supplier. He was so impressed with the success of the no-price system that he offered to sell meat to the restaurant on a no-price basis. Juliano accepted the offer and began setting the meat prices himself. He said he wouldn't think of hurting the supplier by underpricing what he buys.

Juliano flies an American flag outside his restaurant.

The degeneration of American ethics and morality based on fundamental principles is glaringly evident in what employment specialist Robert Half calls time-theft. Half, president of Robert Half International, one of the world's largest financial executive, accounting, and data processing recruiters, says the deliberate and persistent abuse and waste of paid work time by Americans exceeds $150 billion a year.

Half says that time-theft takes a greater toll on American business than all other crimes combined. "Time is our most valuable resource. It cannot be replaced, recovered, or replenished. Employees who willfully waste and misuse time are stealing from their employers," he said. He added that time thieves are a threat to their company, as well as the nation.

Among the most common forms of time-theft revealed by Half's ongoing surveys: habitually arriving late at work, leaving work early, excessive personal telephone calls, nonstop socializing with other employees, feigning illness and taking unwarranted sick leave, taking care of personal business on company time, deliberately working slow in order to create overtime work, reading or watching television during the work period, and operating another business on company time.

Half's latest survey did not include government workers or supervisory personnel. The employees who were surveyed averaged stealing four hours and 22 minutes per week from their employers. One Texas corporation found out that its employees were making over 10,000 telephone calls a month to listen to pornographic recordings.

While there have been no corresponding time-theft studies made in Japan, those who are intimately familiar with Japanese work habits, in both offices and factories, agree that time-theft is far less of a problem in Japan because the Japanese are more diligent in their work and more loyal to their employers.

Quality Control

There is a popular conception in the United States that the Japanese were not concerned about product quality until the idea was introduced to them by Americans following the end of World War II. Until the 1960s, Japan and cheaply made inferior products were virtually synonymous in the American mind. But this image is wrong. Almost all of the cheap toys, cigarette lighters, cameras, wearing apparel, trinkets, and other Japanese-made consumer items that flooded the U.S. in earlier years were imported by Americans who controlled their quality by insisting on the cheapest possible price.

Practically none of these items were sold in Japan. The Japanese would not accept them. This situation continued until Japanese manufacturers and exporters became strong enough to control their own production and eventually their own marketing in the United States. Japanese companies that are now world-famous for the quality of their products were among the first to take over their own marketing in the U.S.

The Japanese discovered quality control, at least on a handicraft basis, well over 1000 years ago. In the 1700s, a Japanese scholar named Toshiaki Honda wrote that every effort should be made by Japanese manufacturers to produce products of the highest possible quality and that this effort should be the cornerstone of the country's national policy.

As Donald Keene notes in his book *The Japanese Discovery of Europe—1720–1830*, the perceptive Mr. Honda went on to say: "In that way, many articles famed for their excellence will be produced in this country. This will help us gain profit when trading with foreign nations."

What the Japanese did soon after the end of World War II was to take advantage of the quality control principles explained to them by American experts working for the Occupation forces in Tokyo and then to invite the noted American quality control authorities, Dr. W. Edward Deming and Dr. J. M. Juran, to Japan to help them revolutionize their quality control system—while American business in general failed to see what was happening.

The Japanese reward effort and spirit, as well as results. In fact, they give precedence to effort and spirit, regardless of the result, and they prefer to be evaluated on these criteria and become resentful when they are not.

For this reason, the Japanese get more pleasure out of the process than the product, and they are particularly motivated to improve the process of anything they undertake. Americans, on the other hand, are not at all enamored of the process of doing anything. "Who cares how you do it as long as you get it done!" is a typical American attitude. We tend to evaluate only results—and we want them right now.

The Japanese worker looks at each product as a challenge to his ability to do better than he has ever done before, to make each product a work of art. The American worker is more likely to do the minimum that is required. It is apparently a part of American culture that doing your very best or making the very best possible product is both a waste of time and money. As a result, we have traditionally accepted a standard that eventually came to be known as AQL or Acceptable Quality Level.

Many American businessmen really did not pick up on the importance of producing quality products until the early 1980s, and only then because of the shocking inroads Japanese companies were making in the American market. It was not until 1981 that Ford and General Motors invited Dr. Deming in to teach them what he had taught the Japanese 30 years before!

The experience of Spectrum Control Inc. of Pennsylvania, profiled in *Inc.* magazine, is typical. The reject rate of one of its products had climbed to 32 percent, and a Japanese company was threatening its market before it finally got serious about changing both its philosophy and its quality control practices. Top management at Spectrum first looked at Japanese quality control techniques and decided they were not suitable for their style of management. Then they studied the statistical control approaches advised by Dr. W. Edward Deming, whose success in Japan has made him a legend. His approach was also considered inappropriate.

Spectrum next went to management consultant Philip Crosby, former director of quality control for ITT, author of *Quality Is Free, Quality Without Tears,* and *The Art of Getting Your Own Sweet Way* and head of Crosby's Quality College in Winter Park, Florida. After going through Crosby's program, the Spectrum management team modified it, adding some of Dr. Deming's techniques, and set up Quality Education System courses for every employee. Posters, leaflets, and memos were used to promote the program. The goal was to achieve zero defects by doing everything right the first time and cleaning up scheduling and other work habits.

Spectrum president Thomas L. Venable said the primary lesson learned from the Japanese, Deming, and Crosby was that zero defects and quality are possible if you have a system that everyone is motivated to follow. So drastic was the change in the work approach at Spectrum that one employee described it as "Like quitting smoking, giving up drinking, and going on a diet—all at the same time!"

By the mid-1980s, most ranking American businessmen had come to the conclusion they had been Japanized enough, that they had learned all they could from the Japanese. They had read dozens of magazine articles and books, listened to lectures, and often made trips to Japan. They knew all about quality circles and teamwork and long-term planning. After all, these were American ideas in the first place. They had just been temporarily misplaced.

I disagree. Most of America's top business leaders and ranking managers have just begun to learn some of the more important lessons the Japanese have to teach. Among these lessons is the idea that businesses have three primary obligations: first, to the people who make up their market; second, to their employees; and third, to their stockholders and—by extension—to the entire country.

Corporate Responsibility

For the most part, America's business leaders think first in terms of their own personal economic and financial well-being. Next, they think of the profitability of their company; and third—finally—they think about those who consume their products or services. Generally speaking, any benefit to the United States is incidental.

American business leaders tend to specialize and they run their companies the same way. They hire or train specialists, put them in specific slots, and leave them there for the rest of their working lives. Many ranking executives in major American companies today have only a general idea of what goes on outside their own offices. They are not only out of touch with their own company, they are out of touch with society.

Of course, there are exceptions. There is a growing number of American businessmen, often self-made entrepreneurs, who have transcended the bounds of capitalistic greed and are now actively engaged in crusades to dramatically raise the living standards of the disadvantaged, to protect the environment, and to use their power to enhance the prospects for world peace.

Three American executives singled out by *U.S. News & World Report* for their various extrabusiness activities were William Norris, chairman of Control Data Corporation; Harold Willens, a Los Angeles real estate mogul; and Robert Anderson, founder and chairman of Atlantic Richfield Company.

Norris combines good business sense with social activism by locating plants, as well as business and technology centers, in inner-city disadvantaged areas, aiding small businessmen and providing educational programs to train uneducated, unqualified people for full-time jobs.

Willens heads up an organization called Business Executives for National Security and spends a considerable amount of his time stumping for nuclear arms control and for using the power of business in a more positive way to ensure the future of the human race.

Anderson founded the Aspen Institute for Humanistic Studies in Colorado, where businessmen meet with scholars, scientists, and artists to discuss social issues and express their views. He helped finance Friends of the Earth, a major U.S. environmental group, and the International Institute for Environment and Development in London. And he has been the catalyst for numerous other efforts to protect the environment.

These men and their kind are still in the minority, however, and are regarded as dangerous mavericks by many of their colleagues, who are frightened by the thought of their corporations having any responsibility beyond profit making.

There are also exceptions on the more traditional corporate level—companies in which management and employees actually communicate with each other, including some in which management and unions actually cooperate with each other to eliminate inefficiencies and boost production. Virtually all of these exceptions have adopted the Japanese concept of quality circles, along with other Japanese management techniques.

F. G. Rodgers, who retired from IBM in 1985 after 34 years as vice president of world marketing, says that the revolution in

American business extends all the way down to the lowest laborers, that more and more Americans *are* taking pride in their work and their company and *are* concerned about corporate responsibility. He says this new attitude is particularly noticeable in attention to small details—more workers are not just putting in time for pay.

Cooperating and Networking

In hard, practical economic terms, it makes a lot more sense for American companies to team up with their Japanese counterparts, instead of trying to beat them in head-on competition. There are, of course, numerous precedents. One area in which Japanese and Americans have worked together especially well is science.

Since 1961, U.S. and Japanese scientists have teamed up in over 300 research projects and over 400 seminars. Some of the more important of these research projects were earthquake engineering, how to detect viruses in salmon eggs, how to prevent the tree disease known as pine wilt, and fusion research.

American companies should especially pursue tie-ups with Japanese companies that are doing advanced research in such areas as ceramics, plastics, fibers, new metals, and weather marketing. This latter field, short- and long-range weather forecasting for specific commercial purposes, has already come a long way in Japan. All the major trading companies, which are active around the world, have their own "global weather men," since lack of rain or too much rain in some distant land has a specific and often extreme effect on the availability and price of many of the agricultural items Japan imports.

A company in Tokyo called Oceanroutes Japan Ltd. provides weather information to a wide range of commercial clients who use it in their planning, as well as in their day-to-day operations. Its clients include shipping companies, travel agencies, TV stations, and oil-drilling operations.

In 1984, the Japan External Trade Organization (JETRO) began setting up Centers for Industrial and Technological Cooperation in five American cities. Earlier in the same year, JETRO joined The Conference Board and Audrey Freedman (marketing consultants) to sponsor the first conference on Japanese-American cooperation in technological research.

Virtually all of the 180 American businessmen who attended the conference were looking for Japanese technological partners.

The Japanese and American patent offices are already sharing patent information that is stored electronically, and plans are underway to implement an automated translation system that would make the information available in other languages. Japan, the United States, and the 11 countries represented by the European Patent Office account for around 80 percent of the world's patent applications.

American companies wanting to get into the China and Southeast Asian markets might consider locating manufacturing facilities in Japan's first free-trade zone in Naha, Okinawa. The Diet approved funding for the zone in March 1986. Enterprises located in the zone will have a number of important advantages, ranging from reductions of or exemptions from customs duties and local taxes to subsidies for the purchase of plant sites. All goods produced in the zone must be shipped out of Japan.

Shanghai, China's largest port city, is only 600 kilometers from the trade zone site. Taiwan is only 500 kilometers away. Detailed information about the trade zone is available from the Okinawa Prefecture Office, 2-6-3 Hirakawa-cho, Tokyo, Japan.

Still, there is substantial resistance among the majority of American businessmen to the idea of forming technological alliances with Japanese companies. Some feel such cooperation would slow progress down instead of boosting it because the competitive factor would be reduced or eliminated. Others say such an alliance would not set well with our European allies.

I see this resistance as primarily a holdover from the provincialism, cultural arrogance, and misplaced nationalism that has traditionally characterized most American businessmen. They must eventually take a global view of themselves and their industries, and such cooperation with Japan and other countries, as well, is a very practical way of becoming truly international.

Of course, especially where Japan is concerned, American companies should make sure they get as much as they give. There is still a strong tendency among Japanese company executives to operate behind closed doors, while expecting a totally open door policy when they visit foreign companies.

Business-to-business cooperation of this type would also be a way of outflanking Japan's solidly entrenched government bureaucrats, particularly many in the Ministry of International Trade and Industry (MITI), who see themselves as modern day Samurai, protecting Japan from economic infiltration and invasion by outsiders.

Just as in the U.S., it is the lower- and middle-level bureaucrats in the government ministries that run them—not the political appointees who serve as their heads. Even the prime minister himself is unable to guarantee that the policies of the government are carried out by these staunchly conservative and strongly nationalistic guardians of Japan.

Another recent phenomenon in American business that has long been used successfully in Japan is networking, not only for new business contacts but specifically to share information and insights on how to overcome business problems. In this case, the Japanese and American approaches differ radically, however. In the U.S., networking is primarily limited to company owners and presidents of nonrelated firms of similar size. The associations are voluntary, and there are no official obligations involved other than keeping the proceedings in the strictest confidence.

These Americans have learned the obvious—that 10 or 15 or 20 good heads are better than one and that the more humanized their approach to business, the more likely they are to succeed.

In Japan, on the other hand, long traditions of secrecy and competition among nonrelated groups resulted in the Japanese limiting their networking to affiliated companies in the same group and to former classmates and alumni brothers.

This is one area where American businessmen have a potential advantage over their Japanese counterparts, if they are wise enough to recognize it and use it. One American professor of management, who is very familiar with the Japanese system, tells his students that if they get nothing else out of their education they should at least make sure they take a dossier of each of their classmates with them into the world of business.

A much more pragmatic and typically American approach to networking is the one being taken by Allan A. Kennedy, president of Selkirk Associates Inc., a Boston computer software company, formerly a management consultant with McKinsey

& Company and co-author of the book *Corporate Cultures*. Kennedy is computerizing the networking concept in a system he calls the Selkirk Networker, which has been described as an "electronic Rolodex."

Users of his system will be able to tap into a nationwide pool of networkers via their computers, making it possible for them to reach large numbers of people who have something in common (membership in the network) and a professed interest in networking. Kennedy notes in *Inc.* magazine that once the number of networkers exceeds a threshhold of some 2,000 users, the productive efficiency of the users will go "right through the roof."

There are growing indications that major American corporations are beginning to develop closer "Japanese-style" relationships with the dozens to hundreds of smaller subcontract firms that supply them. Larger Japanese companies have traditionally used clusters of *shita-uke*, "sub-contractors," or *ko-gaisha*, "child-companies" (subsidiaries), to quickly increase or decrease their production on short notice. Often they virtually run these small companies without being totally responsible for their survival.

General Motors appears to be taking the lead in the development of closer ties between larger American companies and their vendors, ostensibly so it can use the suppliers' products more efficiently. But there is some fear that GM will use its power to weed out the weaker suppliers and that those that survive will become that much more dependent on the whims of GM. David Cole, engineering professor at Michigan University, predicts that this movement will spread rapidly among American manufacturers in general.

NEGOTIATING

The average American businessman is a babe in the woods when it comes to negotiating with the Japanese. He frequently doesn't know enough about his own company. He almost always doesn't know very much about the Japanese company he is dealing with. He is impatient. The faster he can close a deal, the better he thinks he has done. He lays all of his cards on the table immediately and expects the Japanese to understand them as well as he does. He is prepared to discuss them for minutes to hours but can't understand why any discussion should go beyond a few days and why decisions can't be made on the spot or soon thereafter.

Even the largest American companies depend on individuals or small teams of two or three people to handle most negotiations for them. Japanese negotiating teams typically include the managers and submanagers of all the departments concerned. All the managers have done their homework and are able to ask specific questions and give detailed answers. This gives them a practical, as well as a psychological, advantage.

The Japanese are better conditioned culturally and better trained professionally in getting along with people and getting what they want by subtle means. They are polite and humble in mien, but they are patient and persistent and never give up. If they encounter an obstacle, they go around it or under it or outlast it. They appear soft and flexible, but they are very tough and single-minded.

American companies habitually use attorneys to negotiate for them or bring in attorneys as members of their negotiating team—which is one of the reasons we have over 650,000 attorneys in this country. The attorney mentality is anathema to the Japanese (there are fewer than 15,000 attorneys in Japan). Their way of doing business is diametrically opposed to the detailed, legalistic approach practiced by attorneys. They do not deal in absolutes; they do not deal within hard, unchanging, narrowly defined rules. They demand flexibility, room for changing with circumstances.

The top executives in larger Japanese companies almost never do any of the negotiating for their firms. They depend on middle-level managers to do both the staff work and the negotiating, and they step in like the president of a country to sign the agreements after all the work has been done.

We must continue doing business with Japan and should be doing a lot more than we are. It is therefore important that we learn how to negotiate on fairly equal terms with the Japanese. The first lesson is to do our homework. We must learn everything possible about our own companies and the market because we can be sure the Japanese negotiators will know everything. Second, we must learn as much as possible about the Japanese companies we are negotiating with, about the positions and personalities of the individual negotiators, and about the Japanese way of negotiating.

We always want to talk about products, prices, and profits. The Japanese want to learn about the character, personalities, and proclivities of the negotiators and their bosses. Then they want to talk about mutual interests, long-term prospects, company reputation, marketing challenges, the competition, and so on. We must learn how to talk about the things the Japanese want to hear.

The third lesson we should learn from the Japanese is patience. The Japanese do not make snap judgments or instant decisions. Their companies are not run by people who can act individually and quickly. They are operated on a group basis, and groups need a great deal of time to reach a consensus.

American business leaders must become willing to invest more time and money in negotiating with the Japanese. It never ceases to amaze me that an American businessman who is trying to get an agreement with a Japanese company that could means millions of dollars in sales over the years will begrudge the expenditure of a few thousand dollars for travel and hotel expenses to help close the deal—or will get impatient and pull out of the negotiations too soon.

Adopting the Japanese way of negotiation has far wider ramifications than just our dealings with Japan. The same technique is just as effective in negotiating with any company in the U.S. or in the world.

Talking Things Out

The staggering volume of litigation and the huge number of lawyers in the United States today is a major social and economic handicap that is still expanding. Nowadays one can hardly turn around without being threatened by the specter of a lawyer.

I prefer the Japanese system of *chotei*, or "mediation," instead of attorneys and the courts, and I believe most Americans would, too, if they had the opportunity. Many domestic and business problems can be handled by a respected mediator—a go-between who represents both sides dispassionately and gives equitable advice. This does not require an attorney, whose primary interest is most likely to be his fee, not justice.

As for matters actually requiring a knowledge of law, I also recommend that we adopt the Japanese system of using notaries and clerks with some legal training to do most of the work that in the U.S. is handled by attorneys—for considerably lower fees.

Unless the present trend in the United States can be reversed, the country could eventually be choked to death. There are encouraging signs that adaptations of the Japanese system of mediation may save the day.

Several cities in the country—including Cleveland, Oklahoma City, Tucson, Phoenix, Los Angeles, San Jose, and San Francisco—have mediation programs that have become popular alternatives to the court system. Cleveland's system is regarded as a model for other cities.

Mediation can resolve a problem or dispute in one or two hours and cost very little, while a nonjury case can take six to eight months and cost thousands of dollars. A jury case can take years and cost hundreds of thousands of dollars. It is predicted that the mediation system in Phoenix, Arizona, will save the city a quarter of a million dollars annually.

Cases decided by mediation include harassment, trespassing, minor assaults, disturbing the peace, and property disputes. This could be the beginning of the reintroduction of this very simple, sane, and practical social procedure into American life.

As a note of special interest, there are only some 150 foreign lawyers in Japan, most of them American. At this time, only 10 of them are allowed to practice law in Japanese courts. The others act as consultants and help negotiate and draw up contracts. But even this narrow niche may eventually become narrower still, as more and more Japanese law graduates from American universities are hired by major Japanese companies.

Few things so graphically demonstrate the difference between the cultural values of Americans and Japanese as industrial accidents in which people are injured or killed. In the U.S., victims and survivors immediately begin thinking about suing. In the case of major accidents, lawyers flock to the scene like scavengers, competing with each other to line up clients. This sort of behavior is totally reprehensible to the Japanese. They know the company concerned will take responsibility for the accident without being sued and will compensate the victims for their losses to the extent that has become acceptable.

Face to Face

The biggest mistakes that American businessmen have made and continue to make in their efforts to do business with the Japanese is their failure to understand the importance of face-to-face meetings with their Japanese counterparts, and neglecting to follow through.

The Japanese do not like to do business with a disembodied voice that comes in over a telephone line, and, unless the call is from an established customer, generally they will not. They need to see the person they are dealing with, to exchange name cards, get to know him or her, and develop a bond of trust and confidence that cannot be done by phone or letter.

The Japanese depend to a considerable degree on a form of intuitive communication called *haragei*,* or "art of the stomach," in establishing and maintaining working relations with clients and suppliers. This "belly language" requires face-to-face meetings, so the Japanese can almost literally feel the other person out. A person's age, appearance, dress, and all his subtle nuances of behavior play a role in *haragei*.

Japan's social etiquette generally prohibits the use of the Japanese language in a clear, direct, unambiguous way. Often, it is just the opposite. One has to hint at the point he really wants to make, while talking about something else altogether.

Not understanding or appreciating this subtlety of communicating with the Japanese, American businessmen blunder on, making one mistake after the other, and then wonder why they have so many problems making themselves understood and achieving their goals.

There may be no particular need for American businessmen to change their way of doing business with each other, but they certainly need to learn how to use the face-to-face contact and "belly language" when dealing with the Japanese.

Training Americans

Another area in which American business leaders have been misled or have misled themselves is in the operation of their joint ventures or subsidiaries in Japan. Because adult Americans

---

* For more about *haragei* and other aspects of Japanese interpersonal relations and management, see *Japanese Etiquette & Ethics in Business* by Boye De Mente.

find it very difficult to learn the Japanese language and because of numerous other cultural handicaps, they have been overly receptive to the idea that it is better to hire Japanese executives to run their Japan operations for them.

Hiring Japanese managers appears to make a lot of sense, and there are numerous examples where American companies in Japan were unable to succeed *until* they turned management over to Japanese employees. But there are also many weaknesses to this approach, and it is exactly the opposite of what the Japanese have done and are doing in the United States. They have especially large numbers of Japanese managers assigned to their companies in the U.S. and wouldn't think of turning their operations here over to Americans.

Beginning in the 1960s, when competition in Japan began heating up, American companies there began reducing the number of their foreign personnel, citing both rising costs and cultural handicaps. The primary fault with this policy is that it guarantees that American employees of these companies will not learn the Japanese language or how to do business there and puts them in a position of having no choice but to depend on their Japanese employees.

This means that these American companies really do not control whatever market share the companies have. The markets are controlled by their Japanese employees, because in Japan business is done on the basis of personal connections— especially when the proprietor is an absentee foreign owner.

While the number of American businessmen with extensive Japan experience is seriously limited (and many of those who are available are either misused or not used at all), there are tens of thousands of Japanese managers who have spent years in the United States, polishing their language ability, their knowledge of the American way of life, and their ability to do business here.

These individuals are regularly rotated back to their parent companies in Japan, where they join a large and formidable group of colleagues who have had similar experiences abroad— in many countries—and can therefore communicate with each other and with their co-workers still abroad on the basis of firsthand knowledge.

This disparity between the number of Japanese and American businessmen with overseas experience is growing at a rapid rate. And unless American business leaders change their attitudes, the situation will continue to get worse, instead of better. Among other things, the Japanese do not respect any foreign company that chooses not to send its own personnel to Japan. They do, however, appreciate such a situation because they know it allows them to learn virtually all there is to know about American companies and their products and yet keep the advantage of controlling their own market.

The rationale of the American businessman is again based on a short-range view and a strong tendency to take the quick, easy way out. What is most shocking of all is that this attitude appears to be gaining ground among some American firms, despite their many years of experience in Japan.

One of my favorite examples of the differences between the Japanese and American approaches to foreign trade involves a major Japanese trading company. This company, when it first began to plan an advance into Brazil, sent one of its best young managers there for three years to do nothing but learn the language, the life-style, and the method of doing business. Can you imagine any American company committing that much to an individual or even to a country!

Professor Tadao Umesao, director of Japan's National Museum of Ethnology, once described Japan as a "black hole," saying it emitted enormous amounts of energy but did not transmit anything understandable to the outside world. This implies, of course, that Japan absorbs but does not give anything back. Professor Umesao's point is that there is a critical need for Japan to transmit understandable information to the outside world in vast quantities and that it remains semisecluded because of its inability to communicate clearly with the rest of the world.

The professor points out that it is extremely dangerous for Japan to remain hidden behind its language and other cultural barriers and that the country must try to help other nationalities learn the Japanese culture, since a country cannot be understood from its products and foods. Life-style can be exported, he says, but culture cannot. The only way to understand the Japanese is to *share* their culture and get to know them at a level far deeper or beyond their life-style.

One of the most important lessons we still have to learn from the Japanese is that business is first of all a human endeavor.

Until this lesson, in all of its ramifications, is learned and learned well, we will continue to be at a disadvantage in dealing with the Japanese.

For the most part, American businessmen have not had to be sensitive to cultural differences. The American and European market was so big, even though diverse, they were able to treat it as one homogeneous whole that would serve their needs forever. That is no longer the case. Cultural sensitivity and appreciation should be right up there with business administration and accounting if we are going to improve our ability to compete with the Japanese, not to mention the rest of the world.

CHAPTER IX

Living
Japanese
Style

To understand and appreciate the influence the Japanese are having on America, it is necessary to know something about how they live—not only in their factories and offices, but also in their homes and schools. First of all, Japan is a very old country with a highly homogeneous population and culture, while the United States is a very young country with a heterogeneous population from diverse cultures.* Not only does Japan have the world's oldest reigning dynasty (since 660 B.C., according to historical records compiled in 807 A.D.), the Japanese themselves are an ancient people. Recent anthropological evidence indicates that Japanese-like people inhabited the islands some 10,000 years ago.

From 1192 until 1868 Japan was ruled by an elite, hereditary class of sword-carrying (and sword-using!) warriors known as Samurai, which translates, more or less, as "Guards." The principles by which the Samurai class lived and ruled Japan were known as *Bushido* or the Way of the Warrior—and they were strict, indeed. The Samurai had the legal right to

*There is no place on Japanese driver's licenses for color of the hair or eyes.

kill any commoner on the spot if he or she transgressed against the laws and traditions of the land. The Way of the Warrior also called for Samurai to commit suicide rather than lose face or fail in a mission.

Besides a head start of over a thousand years on discipline, group behavior, and other advantageous characteristics, the Japanese also had a spiritual advantage over Christianized Westerners. We claim to have been created by a god in his image. Japanese mythology tells them that they are direct descendants of the gods. That's better than just being made by a god—out of dust!

The Japanese concept of the cosmos is also quite different from that of the West. There is no all-powerful deity who watches over them with a critical eye and a lust for punishing all who stray from a carefully prescribed way of righteousness. To the early Japanese, there were eight million gods (*kami*) of different rank and importance. Everything in nature had its god-spirit and was owed a certain amount of respect and homage. There was even a *kami* for toilets.

The old Japanese universe was divided into three worlds— heaven, earth, and hell—just as it was in the West. But the similarity ended there. The Japanese believed they had to be in harmony with all of the spirits of earthly things in order to stay right with the heavenly deities. Hell was not a frightening possibility to the Japanese, and their gods didn't mind their having fun on earth before they ascended into heaven as spirits.

Trained in these beliefs for centuries, the Japanese have an attitude toward everyday living that is fundamentally different from the attitude of most Americans. Certain aspects of Japanese life are superior to the American equivalent or do not exist in the U.S. at all. And it is my conviction that if they are not being assimilated in the U.S. now, they should be adopted by Americans as rapidly as possible.

HOUSE BEAUTIFUL (AND COMFORTABLE)

There is a growing consensus among American home builders that Americans in the future are going to have to be satisfied with smaller homes on smaller lots, not only because of the cost factor but also because of the growing population and rapidly expanding cities. Here the Japanization of some of our attitudes about living and housing are definitely in order.

The Japanese learned a long time ago to think small and live small because of limited land and building resources. (Although Japan is about the size of the state of Montana in land area, over 80 percent of the country is mountainous, and the entire population, which is about half that of the U.S., lives in a total area of about 23,000 square miles, or the equivalent of one of the larger counties in Arizona, New Mexico, or Texas.)

I remember that in the mid-1950s, when the population of Japan was 72 million, economists, sociologists, psychologists, and politicians were predicting that Japan could not survive if the population went beyond 85 or 90 million. The population now is over 120 million, and the survival of the Japanese has not been threatened. People are far more adaptable than they are generally given credit for, and we do not have to give up any quality of life to adjust to smaller houses and less living space.

One of the first things we could do is cut down on the amount and size of the permanent furnishings we put into our homes. Most American homes have a dining room table, a kitchen table, and a coffee table. Each of these tables now serves a slightly different purpose, but one would be enough to take care of all of our needs.

Our homes have one or more sofas and anywhere from a few to dozens of chairs, all of which take up a substantial amount of floor space at all times. Japan's versatile *zabuton* (floor cushions) could replace all of these, but we don't have to go that far. We could come up with seating arrangements that could be put away when not in use.

Early homes in rural areas of Japan were expected to last for hundreds of years and to accommodate several families. They were built with a great deal of flexibility, allowing the various rooms to be used as bedrooms, living rooms, and even workrooms, as the occasion required.

With the rising cost of construction making it increasingly difficult for newly wedded Americans to afford their own houses, it might be time for us to begin building homes that will accommodate—or can be readily adapted to accommodate—two or more nuclear families. There would be numerous social, as well as economic benefits, from going back to this old way of living.

The first thing the foreign visitor to a traditional Japanese house learns is that shoes are not worn inside the house. Each house or apartment has a specially designed vestibule area, called *genkan* (gane-khan), where shoes are stored when not in use, put on when leaving the house, and removed upon returning.

The custom of removing shoes before entering a home was well established in ancient times as a sanitary measure. After the appearance of *tatami* reed-mat floors several hundred years ago, it would have been especially unthinkable to track in dust, mud, and other refuse from the outside.

This Japanese concern for cleanliness and neatness is rooted in Shintoism, the native religion of Japan, which equates cleanliness with godliness. The philosophy of Zen Buddhism, imported from China in the twelfth and thirteenth centuries, also brought with it a strong belief in physical, as well as mental, tidiness. Zen novices have traditionally set out on the long road to enlightenment by learning how to sweep, mop, and wash.

Most Americans, on the other hand, continue to treat their homes as if they were dirt-floor hovels, caves, or animal stalls, and think about taking their shoes off at the doorway only if they are dripping wet or smeared with mud. It never ceases to amaze me that people who cover their floors with wall-to-wall carpeting—and sometimes white carpeting at that—continue to wear their outside shoes inside, with little or no effort to clean their footwear before entering their homes.

The idea of removing one's shoes before entering a carpeted home is very simple, but it never occurs to most Americans. When the concept is suggested by someone who has been Japanized, he or she is likely to get anything from a horselaugh to a sneer. Some people react as if the notion were un-American and give the impression they would get ugly if the idea were pushed.

Regardless of whether we carpet our floors, it makes no sense to track dust and other grime into our homes, no matter how rustic they may be. I vote that all the rule books be revised, making the removal of shoes at doorways not only acceptable but expected.

The Japanese influence in home fashions or interior decoration in the United States dates back to the late 1800s, when importers and affluent travelers began to bring in Japanese windscreens, tables, chests, fabrics, porcelains, lacquerware, and shoji panels. The attraction of Japanese furnishings and decorations is found in their classic shapes, the harmonious blending of colors, the refinement of their beauty, and the aura of calm, almost spiritual tranquility they impart.

In the fall of 1984, Bloomingdale's, one of the oldest and most famous retail store chains in the U.S., sponsored a large-scale promotion of Japanese products, complete with background displays and handicraft artists, to showcase the merchandise in its natural environment. The idea was to portray contemporary Japan as enriched by its cultural heritage—to capture the essence of Japan. "There is a growing interest in the U.S. in Japanese products other than cars and electronics and in the traditional manifestations of Japanese culture," said a Bloomingdale spokesman.

Futon

The invention of the elevated bed was a boon to mankind when the floors of sleeping quarters were alive with creeping and crawling things or were wet and cold. The idea of building sleeping platforms on stilts probably grew out of the instinct that goes back to the days when our ancestors slept in trees and no doubt at some stage fashioned crude, latticed pads of intertwined branches covered with leaves.

Those of us who are still less civilized, less evolved culturally and philosophically, are still motivated by a deep, subconscious urge to seek out a higher place when we bed down. We may now rationalize this instinct by claiming that sleeping on a raised platform is more comfortable than sleeping on the floor or ground-level. But, of course, that is nonsense.

The Japanese apparently sprang from different trees because they developed a different relationship with their environment very early in their history. This different relationship led to the development of raising the entire house several inches off the ground (for ventilation and to avoid placing their wooden building materials in contact with the ground). At first, the floors were covered with thin straw mats. Eventually, they developed a thick, soft reed mat called *tatami,* which became the traditional flooring for houses.

There was a strict demarcation between the outside and the inside of a house. Footgear worn on the outside was never worn on the inside. Floors were kept scrupulously clean by daily dusting, wiping, and scrubbing. People sat on, ate on, and slept on the floors of their homes.

In earlier times, people slept on and under straw mats and "quilts" made for that purpose. After the discovery and development of durable cloth fibers and the appearance of cloth-covered sitting cushions, it gradually became customary to make bedding out of the same materials. Thus the now traditional *futon* (fuu-tone) came into existence.

The futon bed is a perfect complement to the traditional Japanese home, with its reed-mat floors, fragile rice-paper doors, and wall panels. The mats are not made to sustain heavy, legged furniture and the houses are generally too small to accommodate massive, permanently placed furnishings. The pallet-type bedding that could be spread out on the floor and taken up in a few seconds was thus a very rational and practical approach to sleeping facilities.

The futon concept began to catch on in the U.S. in the 1960s among young people who couldn't afford expensive furniture, often didn't have space for it, and were looking for a simpler life-style. The trend is continuing to gain adherents, especially among the young, who do not see futon as that different from sleeping bags.

For the typical older, bed-trained and -conditioned American, the thought of switching from a large, solid wood or metal bed to some relatively thin mattresses and quilts spread on the floor brings on some rather interesting psychological reactions. I predict, however, that the futon concept will continue to make inroads in the U.S., if for no other reason than it is eminently practical for young people just starting out in housekeeping in small apartments.

The American entrepreneurs who have developed a sofa/futon, actually a sofa-couch that unfolds into a bed, have gone too far. Their sofa/futon is very attractive but it no longer has the practical, convenient qualities of the true futon. Theirs is simply a sofa bed with a mattress that is called a futon.

Futon have several advantages over beds. They cost much less. When not in use, you can take them up and use the space for other purposes. You can bed down several people in the same room just by spreading additional futon around on the floor. They are also much more practical for sexual activity because they provide a more stable base than a spring mattress does.

Incense

The ancient Japanese custom of *koh-do*, or incense appreciation—which, writer Lou Garcia says, "creates a feeling of tranquility and a dimension of graceful living that opens up a whole new world of spiritual awareness and understanding"—would seem to be one of the many traditional Japanese practices least likely to find a positive reception in the U.S.

There have been a few devotees of the art of *koh-do* in the United States since before the turn of the century, but a series of *koh-do* ceremonies presented in 20 American cities in 1983—and the resulting publicity—introduced the custom to thousands of Americans.

The *koh-do* ceremony was brought to Japan from China in the eighth century by Buddhist monks who used the mystical aromas in their religious ceremonies to achieve spiritual enlightenment. Gradually, the practice spread to Court nobles in Kyoto. Adds Garcia: "They would amuse themselves trying to identify a wide variety of delicate and subtle scents from the deep forests of Japan, as well as from Southeast Asia, 'listening' to their fragrances, as a way of pampering their moods and creating imaginary scenes for their poetry and plays."

In the fourteenth century, Japan's elite Samurai warriors began using incense to perfume their helmets and armor as a way of expressing their cultural achievements and dignity. The appreciation of incense reached its zenith in the seventeenth and eighteenth centuries, when it was adopted by the upper and middle classes of Japan.

American practitioners of *koh-do* use it to enhance the ambience of their home or office, finding it a very pleasant way to relax the mind and soothe nerves jangled by the demands of industrialized life.

The Neiman-Marcus chain of stores was instrumental in helping popularize *koh-do* in the U.S. The company first began carrying incense in 1983 in its West Coast stores, but the interest was so great that it soon appeared in all N-M outlets across the country. The world's largest manufacturer of incense, Nippon Kodo, created a new scent called Scentsual especially for Neiman-Marcus. In the meantime, other stores, including Bloomingdale's and I. Magnin, now carry incense.

Incense appreciation has a pronounced quieting and mind-expanding effect on those who find the fragrances agreeable. Perhaps its widespread use in the U.S. would help reduce the level of violence that plagues the country.

Toilets

Traditionally styled Japanese toilets are in a class by themselves and have been a popular subject in literature and entertainment for centuries. In the 1960s, a book entitled *President of the Toilets* became a best-seller. The Japanese word for toilet, *Obenjo*, literally means "Honorable Convenient Place," which makes a lot of sense.

For centuries, Japanese toilets consisted of deep pits beneath homes and buildings. The toilets were usually situated at the end of a hallway on a side of the building accessible from a garden or lane and enclosed in a tiny room. The pits beneath the toilet rooms were floored over, with a narrow opening in the floor that was capped with a solid wooden lid when the toilet was not in use. Although the toilets were kept scrupulously clean, they became pungently aromatic during the spring, summer, and fall months; and, for someone not used to them, they were a very heady experience.

There is an important benefit to be gained from the floor-level Japanese *Obenjo*. It is far more natural and healthy for us to squat in order to defecate, instead of perching ourselves on an elevated seat. Squatting is something that human beings have been doing since well before they jumped down out of the trees and began running around more or less upright. Squatting is therefore a natural action and a natural position.

DINING AND ENTERTAINING

Americans are rapidly developing a taste for traditional Japanese foods, including raw fish. Food prejudices are among the most powerful influences affecting our lives. To deliberately alter them often requires a great deal of courage, maturity, and fortitude. The mere mention of raw fish is enough to make many Americans start gagging. Among the unsophisticated, it is also likely to reinforce the stereotype that despite their technological advances, the Japanese are still an uncivilized and primitive people.

The traditional Japanese diet of grains, vegetables, fruit, and seafood turns out to be the optimum diet for a long, healthy life. Furthermore, it is my position, at least, that eating sashimi (small pieces of raw fish) and sushi (slices of raw fish and other seafoods on buns of rice) is both a gourmet experience and a conspicuous improvement in one's diet.

I must confess that my own first experience with raw fish was a good example of the power food has over us. The only way I could take it was to follow each bite with a swig of beer. By the time the meal was over, I could have eaten a live fish! The second time, however, I was able to cut down on the amount of beer, and the third time, beer was an accessory, not a necessity.

Eating

The raw-fish prejudice of most Americans is reinforced by our noses. We cannot separate the smell of rotting fish, especially freshwater fish, from the idea of the taste of raw fish. The raw fish that the Japanese and other aficionados eat does not have a "fishy" taste or smell. Fresh raw fish, particularly salt-water fish, actually has very little smell. The taste varies, of course, with the kind of fish, and it is impossible to describe since it is totally unique. But whatever the kind of fish, the taste is clean, fresh, and crisp, and it has its own distinctive flavor.

Maguro (tuna), probably the most popular of all the raw-fish treats, has a taste that is often described as "sweet," but it is not a cloying, sugar sweetness and does not overpower the palate as sugar does. Raw fish is almost never eaten by itself (just as we almost never eat ham or turkey or cheese by themselves). It is especially complemented by mildly vinegared rice, a slightly salty soy sauce (shoyu), tiny bits of fresh ginger, and beer.

We now know that cooking alters not only the taste of foods but their contents, as well, often destroying the vitamins and minerals they contain and sometimes creating carcinogens from otherwise harmless elements. It is therefore healthier and safer to eat uncontaminated fresh fish raw than cooked.

This is not to say that everyone will necessarily like the taste of raw fish or that everyone should be expected to eat it. Some people can't stand the taste of bread or potatoes or other traditional American staples. What I am saying is that a surprising percentage of the people who try sashimi and sushi quickly develop a taste for it and become enthusiasts. And having done so, they can be proud of having eliminated an irrational hangup and taken a step toward a healthier mind and body.

Over the next decade, the number of sushi shops operated by just one company in the United States is expected to number from 1,000 to 2,000. The company is a joint venture between Japan's Sun Atom Company, which manufactures a microcomputer-operated sushi shop management system, and New Meiji Franchise Corporation, a major Japanese food chain. The first of the computerized sushi shops opened in Los Angeles in 1984, just in time for the Summer Olympics.

I wouldn't be surprised to see as many as 20 or 30 percent of all adult Americans eating sushi as part of their regular diet within 10 or 15 years. Sushi is clean, attractive, and simple to prepare, and it has a unique taste that quickly grows on one. It remains the top "convenience" food in Japan, despite the extraordinary inroads made by hamburgers since the 1970s.

As with most traditional Japanese foods, there is a special mystique surrounding the preparation and eating of sushi. Until 1984, women were more or less officially barred from the profession of sushi making. It was felt that their "warm, cosmetic-smelling hands" would spoil the delicate taste of the dish. Much to the surprise of many, the offering of one- and two-year courses in sushi making to women, as well as men, at the Sushi Academy Gakuin, which opened in Tokyo in 1984, has not had any discernably adverse effect on either the taste or popularity of sushi.

Most of the sushi chefs working in Japanese restaurants in the United States are graduates of Sushi University, established in Tokyo in 1980. Students attend SU for three to six months. Classes cover the history of sushi, how to shop for the best and freshest ingredients, handling the tools of the trade, and running a sushi shop. Students also learn how to make Americanized sushi that include avocado, imitation crab meat, etc., and to use stronger sweet, spicy, and salty flavors to fit the American palate. Since Japanese sushi restaurants in the U.S. have to offer other dishes as well, students at SU also learn how to make sukiyaki, teriyaki, tempura, and various noodle dishes.

Prior to the opening of these schools, men had to serve under a master for seven or more years in order to become journeymen in sushi shops.

Other Japanese foods that are gaining in popularity in the U.S. are various noodle dishes, rice dishes, rice crackers, seaweed and kelp, and tofu (soy bean curd).

Another very special Japanese dish that should be immediately adopted in the U.S. is eels. Yes! Those squirmy things that look like snakes. The Japanese, who eat over 300 million eels a year, believe that they are an aphrodisiac and contribute to overall physical stamina. They are most popular in summer and are generally broiled, covered with a sweet soy-based sauce, and eaten with rice. The two most popular dishes are *unagi-domburi* (a bowl of rice topped with sections of eel), and *unagi-teishoku* (a bowl of rice and eel, along with an eel-based broth and various pickles).

Eels are very high in calcium and have more vitamin A, B1, B2, and E than meat or fish. Cooked and served Japanese style, eels have a rich, piquant taste that reminds me of eggplant. They can be raised in acquaculture farms in a relatively simple process that lends itself to mass production, and they would be a marvelous addition to the American diet.

Another popular Japanese dish that immediately goes over with most Americans—and one that could give hamburgers a run for their money—is *yaki-tori*, or charcoal broiled chicken. In this case, it is small chunks of chicken, along with slices of onion and green pepper (quail eggs and calf's liver are optional), skewered on metal or bamboo sticks, seasoned with salt or soy sauce, and broiled over an open flame. *Yaki-tori* is easy to prepare, convenient to eat, and inexpensive, and it appeals to most palates—making it ideal as a snack or main course.

The most commonly eaten Japanese food (not counting rice) is probably some variety of noodle dish—soba, udon, ramen—in a delicious soup stock, usually garnished with bits of vegetables, meats, chicken, or eggs in various combinations. It generally takes Westerners some time to develop a taste for

Japanese-style noodles, mainly because of the soup stock, which usually contains soy sauce and the essence of fish, but again the taste is distinctive and quickly grows on one.

Noodle dishes have a long and important history in Japan. They are easy to prepare, nutritious, and relatively inexpensive. Soba made of buckwheat has been associated with good health and longevity for centuries. Until recently, virtually every Japanese ate buckwheat soba during the last week of each year as a means of ensuring that they would be healthy and live through the following year. The custom is still popular, and soba shops do a significant percentage of their business during the last week in December. Because of the growing interest in health in the U.S., the proven nutritional value of buckwheat, and the attraction of Japanese food, I believe it is only a matter of time before soba, udon, and other Japanese noodle dishes will be everyday fare in America.

In the early 1980s, Japan's Ise Group, a large dealer in eggs, established a subsidiary in the U.S. called Life Design Japan Inc. to sell Japanese health foods door to door. Life Design Japan utilizes American college students and housewives to do their selling. The company gives the students loans to pay for their education, with the proviso that they repay the loans by selling the company's health food products. The foods are snack items high in vitamins C and E, along with vegetable fiber.

Japanese food may start out as a challenge and a novelty to Americans, but it quickly develops into something that borders on an obsession. Japanese food is distinctive in both appearance and taste. It is attractive and pure in the sense that you can recognize what it is. It looks and tastes clean. Once you have developed a taste for it, the addiction never goes away, and you crave it and feel unfulfilled if you are unable to eat it fairly often.

Japanese food has been described as modular, meaning it is made to fit together and form an aesthetically pleasing pattern. Every little piece of traditional fare has its own individual shape, size, color harmony, and balance. Each piece is to be eaten separately and savored for its own identity and taste.

The Japanese food phenomenon has just begun in the United States. If you want to see into the future, visit the business district in the east 40s, between 47th and 49th streets, in New York City. This two-block area is packed with Japanese restaurants that range from plain, tiny diners to posh, exclusive places patronized by the elite of the city's Japanese business community and large numbers of Japanized Americans.

One of the most popular restaurants in the district is the Hatsuhana, whose parent company got its start in the Diet (Parliament) Building in Tokyo, where you had to be a member of the Diet to get in. The bilevel place in New York has modernized Japanese decor. Hatsuhana specializes in sashimi (raw fish) and sushi (raw fish on vinegared rice buns), which represent the epitome of traditional Japanese cuisine.

Other popular Japanese restaurants in this same area are Chikubu (sashimi, sushi, noodles, eel and salmon teriyaki) and Takesushi, where the specialty is imported fugu, or blowfish (with the poison removed before it leaves Japan). Sushi and sashimi as also big at Takesushi.

The important thing is to note the percentage of the customers that are not Japanese and to learn that the number of Americans patronizing the area is growing steadily.

Some Dining Customs

One of the most delightful of all Japanese customs is that of providing guests with small, dampened hand-and-face cloths upon their arrival at inns and at many bars and higher class restaurants. These washcloths, called *Oshibori*, are generally chilled in the summer and heated in the winter (there are especially designed hot/cold "ovens" for this purpose). In some places of business, the *Oshibori* are soaked in water to which has been added essence of jasmine or some other pleasant aroma.

Whether it is winter or summer or anywhere in between, being presented an Oshibori as soon as you sit down in a restaurant is one of the most pleasant customs ever devised by man. The dampened and sometimes aromatic towel is both soothing and cleansing. It provides instant refreshment that relaxes you and prepares you both physically and emotionally for the food or drink or conversation that is to follow.

A few Americans have adopted the *Oshibori* custom in their own homes, and a few businesses have picked up on the idea. I strongly recommend that people everywhere begin asking for *Oshibori* when they go into any kind of eating or drinking place—and not be satisfied with those tiny little fingertip "towels" dispensed in paper envelopes by some airlines!

The adoption of the *Oshibori* in the United States would not put anybody out of work. On the contrary, it would create a huge market for *Oshibori* towels and for the equipment needed to prepare and serve them. Just as important, it would add to the quality of life in this country and help make all of us a little more civilized.

In traditionally styled Japanese homes and restaurants, the customary seat of honor (*kami-za*), given to guests and the most senior member of the family or group, is the one nearest the *tokonoma*, or "beauty alcove," that graces living rooms and *ryotei*, restaurant dining rooms. The *tokonoma* is usually away from the door, near the "head" of the room. The custom allows the Japanese to pay special respect to individuals on all mealtime occasions and adds something to the ambience and order of life that we might do well to emulate.

In the desk and chair arrangements of virtually all Japanese offices, meeting rooms, etc., there is an obvious "head" place assigned to the ranking individual, which establishes the hierarchy and is plain for all to see. This system is practical and useful in business and adds a special touch of decorum to private settings. While we do not have the *tokonoma* to denote a seat of honor, virtually all tables have a "head," which can be used for the same purpose.

Japanese and American attitudes are often diametrically opposed to each other, and questions of which is "right" or "wrong" often create spirited debate. These philosophical and cultural differences are especially common where human relationships are concerned.

One of my first lessons in this area occurred shortly after my arrival in Japan in the late 1940s. A Japanese employee was instructed to make arrangements for a party at a local inn. He asked for a sum of money to tip the inn employees in advance. I asked him why he wanted to give the tip before we had the party and explained that it was the American custom to tip after the fact.

"If you want good service, you must tip in advance. Otherwise, how can you expect the staff to provide you with any service beyond the minimum?" he replied.

It took no great brain to understand and appreciate this logic. But there is more to the philosophy and practice of tipping in Japan that is even more interesting. Direct tipping of an individual is not common in Japan because it contradicts the traditional Japanese concept of service. In their view, a customer is a guest (the word for customer and guest—*okyaku*—is the same), and everyone is entitled to the best possible service as a matter of maintaining proper human relations. The idea that people should be paid extra for fulfilling this obligation verges on being insulting. There is also, of course, the recognition that people respond positively and favorably to service beyond what is expected.

Tipping in advance is not that common in Japan now, but what has become fairly universal among hotels and higher-class restaurants is the practice of adding a "service charge" onto the regular charges, ostensibly in lieu of direct tipping. These surcharges are not passed on directly to employees. The official word is that the company or proprietor uses this extra income to help pay for the overall benefits provided to all employees. Despite the fact that you know you are paying extra in the form of the service charges, they are easier to ignore than direct tips.

In Japanese hotels and first-class restaurants, employees are generally forbidden to accept tips and are instructed to return them when given. Not being expected to tip taxi drivers (unless they do something really out of the ordinary for you), and not being expected to leave tips in restaurants—no matter what the class or degree of service—is a marvelous feeling that contrasts sharply with the effect the American tipping system has on most people.

There is something basically unsettling about any business in which people are expected to make a significant percentage of their income from tips—especially tips that are supposedly given in recognition of special service that generally is not received. I propose that all Americans take a cue from the Japanese and immediately repudiate the present system of tipping. Employees should insist on being paid a decent wage, and patrons should hereafter tip only on very special occasions.

Partying

At parties, formal dinners, and other social gatherings in Japan it is common for participants to be asked to put on some kind of entertaining performance—singing, dancing, recitation, and so on. Since this is an established custom, all Japanese are naturally aware of it, and most of them are able to come through. Many of them have secretly, or at least discreetly, polished a particular skill to the point that they are quite good. This "hidden talent" is known in Japanese as *kakushi gei*, and everyone is automatically expected to have one. On numerous occasions, I have been put in extremely embarrassing situations by being called on to display a *kakushi gei* I did not have.

Of course, my hosts had no intention of embarrassing me. They assumed without thinking that I could do *something* in public that was entertaining. Now there is a new wrinkle in this cultural custom that has made it even more important for visiting businessmen to have a *kakushi gei*. A significant percentage of all businessmen in the country now regularly put on solo, as well as duo or group, singing performances in the various bars they attend on a regular basis. These performances are known as *karaoke*, which refers to singing into a microphone hooked up to a musical sound system that plays the song of your choice. *Karaoke* is short for "empty orchestra" and only requires that you provide the vocal contribution.

The need for emotional self-expression is a powerful influence in the Japanese character, and the popularity of *karaoke* singing in bars and cabarets by male patrons is one of the strongest manifestations of this need. Indeed, it is a marvelous way to express emotions, as well as fulfilling other basic needs.

After more than 30 years experience in Japan, during which time I invariably begged off participating in such public exhibitions, I finally, on my most recent visit to Tokyo, allowed myself to be virtually dragged to the microphone in a small cabaret and did my best to sing a popular American song. I didn't know the words, so I tried to read them from a songbook provided by the cabaret.

I was genuinely surprised that I finally managed to dredge up the courage to embarrass myself in front of an audience. I was even more surprised at the emotional kick I got out of the effort, miserable though it was. My host that evening was the dignified president of a Japanese company who insisted that I could understand the meaning and importance of *karaoke* only if I did it myself. He was right. I was in fact so impressed that I later promised the president I would learn the words of two or three songs and put on a much better performance the next time I was in Tokyo.

For most Japanese businessmen, *karaoke* has taken the place of poetry and various other artistic skills expected of all Japanese. It qualifies as a *shumi*, which is usually translated as "hobby" but actually means something like "tastes." The Japanese do not feel intellectually or spiritually complete until they have gained some skill in an art, and *karaoke* serves very nicely.

I would like to see *karaoke* become a universal practice in the United States. Ideally everyone would learn a *kakushi gei* in childhood. But, since most of us did not, or have long since forgotten whatever art we may have learned, the next best thing is for us to begin hosting *kakushi gei* parties, and warn those who are invited well in advance, so they have time to come up with an act. This would add considerably to our cultural achievements and make our social life a lot more fun. Anything that would improve on parties where people stand around drinking and talking would be a welcome change. The practice should spread rapidly since we already have a tradition of singing along with piano players at bars.

Karaoke in fact has already gained a toehold in the U.S. The first "karaoke mikes," made by the Japanese company Uniden, were brought into the U.S. in the early 1980s. These "mikes" were called "Extend-A-Song." In 1984, approximately 25,000 units were sold here. The device mixes the singer's voice and a prerecorded orchestra through a powerful 20-watt speaker and has the same enhancement features (reverberation) that are used in recording studios. A second built-in cassette deck records your performance, and you can make duplicate tapes at the touch of a button.

One of the most interesting annual customs in Japan is the *Bonenkai*, or "Forget the Year Parties," some of which are held as early as the middle of December. At first glance, these parties may appear to be similar to our pre-Christmas parties or the "Thank God It's Friday" celebration, but they are more than a Christmas get-together or an expression of relief that another week of work is over.

Essentially, *bonenkai* parties consist of drinking, eating, and having a good time with family members, friends, and co-workers, including, of course, those you had runs-ins with during the year. There are no explicit apologies or expressions of forgiveness. All this is expressed by your presence and participation in the party.

It might seem on the surface that our own traditional New Year's Eve parties serve the same function as the *bonenkai*. But they are not quite the same. They are to celebrate the beginning of the new year with family and friends, and nothing more. There is no thought of their having any other content or purpose. And that is where the difference and the importance lie.

The *bonenkai* have a much deeper, therapeutic purpose, and they are one of the many facets of the Japanese way of maintaining social harmony in the workplace, as well as the home. The specific connotation of *bonenkai* is "party to forget all the bad things that happened during the year." This means not only to forget all of your own mistakes, embarrassing moments, and other face- and ego-damaging experiences, but also to forget all the transgressions against you by others. If the absolution is complete, you are able to start the new year with a totally clean slate, with no mental baggage hanging over.

CHAPTER X

Loving and Learning Japanese Style

J apanese-style Zen was first introduced into the United States in 1906, when Soyen Shaku's *Sermons of a Buddhist Abbot* was published in Chicago by Open Court Press. But it hasn't got very far and it is still misunderstood and misused. It deserves a far better and wider reception than it has received.

The philosophy and early principles of Zen originated in India in the sixth century A.D. by a monk named Bodhidharma. Unhappy with the way he and his Buddhist followers were being treated in his own home country, Bodhidharma left for China. Arriving there sometime around 520, he also immediately got into trouble with a local provincial lord who told him to leave town. Traveling northward, Bodhidharma was finally welcomed at a Shaolin Temple, where he sat facing a wall and meditating for nine years.

At the end of this search for enlightenment, Bod was said to be so in tune with nature that he could hear the conversation of ants. Thereafter, Zen Buddhism flourished in China.

Zen was first introduced into Japan from China by the Buddhist priest Eisai (1141–1215), who was followed by another famous Zen advocate, Dogen (1200–1253). The Zen philosophy, with its strict physical and mental disciplines, was quickly adopted by the leaders of the Shogunate government in Kamakura, as well as the professional military families who were to become known as Samurai.

In the centuries that followed, Zen precepts seeped into Japan's total culture, influencing the language, psychology, arts, crafts, personal relationships, and conduct of business and war.

In its simplest form, Zen is a way of gaining control of the body and mind. The ultimate goal is to be able to recognize the difference between illusion and reality, between what is true and what is false, and, thereafter, to conduct one's life according to strict principles of simplicity, austerity, and oneness with nature.

Like most other disciplines, Zen is subject to being subverted to various uses, such as improving fighting skills and hardening one's self to the rigors of war. The Samurai, for example, used Zen to help them develop incredible ability with the sword. Some of the masters became so skilled they could not be defeated in one-on-one combat.

I recommend that Zen study and practice be made a part of the educational system in the United States for several reasons. Zen novices are required to sit still, without moving or making any sound for extensive periods of time every day. This would be excellent discipline for children, even if they did nothing else. As the children got older, the period of required stillness would force them to confront their own minds, their own inner selves, which would encourage the development of maturity and wisdom, reduce tension, and improve their behavior—or at least give them less time to get into trouble.

Since the benefits of meditating have been pretty much accepted by a large number of American adults, adding Zen principles to the practice of meditating would not be such an evolutionary leap, and the rewards would be significant. The principles of Zen are readily available in a number of good books, and the knowledge is free for the taking.

If Zen were the only factor in the Japanization of America and went far enough, the influence would be both profound and pervasive, altering the character and course of our history in a very positive way.

SEX JAPANESE STYLE

In the late 1940s in Tokyo, I began dating an 18-year-old Japanese girl whom I had met in a restaurant. A few weeks later she invited me to her home, where I met her mother and 13-year-old sister.

Not long thereafter, I stayed at the girl's house on a Saturday night. On Sunday morning, the young sister came into my room, showed me a sex-position chart that depicted, in color, virtually every conceivable way a couple could engage in sex, and asked me which position I liked best. I was embarrassed and tried to joke my way out of the situation by saying I liked them all. The chart had been given to the girl's mother when she got married and was in keeping with a long tradition of sexual openness in Japan.

Unlike Christian-dominated Westerners, whose sexual attitudes and behavior are the warped products of a stern, male-run church, the Japanese have never regarded sex as a moral or religious issue. There was outrageous sexual discrimination against women during Japan's long feudal age, but, generally speaking, the Japanese were never subjected to the sexual restraints and taboos that caused so much suffering, so many ruined lives, as in the West—until they began imitating the West, that is.

There is a conspicuous feminine flavor to Japanese customs and life-styles, a flavor that has grown out of centuries of emphasis on refinement in literature, the arts, and other cultural pursuits. This same feminizing process has been very conspicuous in the U.S. since the 1960s, and the stronger the Japanese influence, the stronger the trend is likely to become.

We have made great progress in recent decades in getting sex away from the church and the government, and we believe there is now very little that we can learn from contemporary Japan about sex. There are, however, a number of old Japanese customs pertaining to male-female relations that I believe we should socially and legally sanction and then encourage their development. These include trial marriages and matchmaking.

Go-Betweening

Approximately one-quarter of all marriages that take place in Japan are still *Omiai*—arranged by marriage bureaus and other types of middlemen and women, including the presidents, other executives, and managers of departments and sections in companies. The system has been brought up to date, however, with computer readouts and videotapes of eligible brides and grooms.

A German company, Altmann System International, is the oldest and largest computerized *Omiai* company in Japan. There are dozens of other companies and thousands of individuals who act as *nakodo*, or matchmakers. Many major Japanese firms provide substantial financial support to their own corporate matchmaker clubs.

The marriage service maintained by a member of the prestigious Mitsubishi Group is called the Diamond Family Club. Company employees who want to make use of the service go to the club's special office, where they fill out questionnaires about their lives, interests, and preferences in a mate (while such songs as "By the Time I Get to Phoenix" and "Bridge over Troubled Water" are piped into the interview rooms). They are then given a list of 10 male or female fellow employees who are also seeking mates. Participants are forbidden to date more than one potential partner at a time.

In larger Japanese companies, male employees who are not married by the age of 30 come under increasing pressure from their superiors to find mates. Many such companies will not send unmarried managers overseas. Male employees who expect to rise to senior positions within the company know that remaining single past the age of 30 can become a serious handicap.

In companies that have corporate marriage agencies, someone in most major departments is usually charged with the responsibility for encouraging unmarried employees to make use of the service.

Tsuri Kaki (marriage data on the individual) is an important part of the records of matchmakers—on an individual, as well as a corporate, basis—which we already have in our own dating and matchmaking clubs. But I believe we should go further. I believe that something similar to the Japanese institution of the *nakodo* has a place in the United States and should be formally adopted.

Ideally, an older friend of one of the families or a professional go-between would either volunteer or be appointed to act as the sponsor, to help find a suitable mate when this kind of help is needed. The go-between could also become the godfather or godmother to the couple thereafter, to watch over them, help them make difficult decisions, mediate conflicts, and take them to task for destructive behavior.

Our present hit-and-miss method of meeting and marrying needs a backup. The marriage arranger has been a well-known and popular figure in many Western societies for centuries, and formally introducing the position into the U.S. could result in a substantial improvement in the quality of family life and life in general.

A saying often heard in Japan today is "In Japan, love begins with marriage." In the United States, the idea that love ends with marriage is certainly not always true, but it does point up a significant weakness in our present system.

The U.S. especially needs the *nakodo* system for older people who have already been married and divorced—or widowed—as well as for younger people who are not able to find acceptable mates on their own.

Practicing Husbands (and Wives)

Trial marriages, commonplace in premodern Japan, when the man was known as *nai-in no otto* or "practicing husband," are something that I would like to see revived in Japan, as well as imported into the United States and fully sanctioned by all the institutions that involve themselves in the private conduct of people at large.

The custom is very simple. A man and woman who are sufficiently interested in each other to consider marriage set up housekeeping for a specific period of time to see if they can make a go of it. If the trial period is a success, the couple marries. If not, they go their separate ways. One important criterion for a trial marriage should be that both parties in the arrangement be fully informed on the subject of birth control and make a firm commitment to follow the most effective methods.

Unofficial trial marriages, already practiced in the U.S. today on a rapidly growing scale, take a great deal of the guesswork, heartache, family violence, and child abuse out of American marriages, since most housekeeping couples know within six months or so if they have made a mistake. Professor Howard van Zandt, an Old Japan-Hand, points out that our Colonial ancestors practiced trial marriages, with marriage following only after the young woman became pregnant.

We should reintroduce the practice, improving on both the early American and Japanese systems. To be as effective as possible, such sanctioned trial marriages should be for six months to one year. The minimum period would help weed out people who aren't serious or who are unsuited for each other, and a year should be enough time for them to decide if they want to make it permanent.

In days past, the primary obstacle to adopting a system of trial marriages was the old religious myth that sexual intercourse is immoral and sinful, except between legally married couples. Most people, including many who are devout members of organized religions, have finally recognized that all attempts to control sexual behavior are political, not moral, and that sex is nothing more than a physical act that can be intensely pleasurable, as well as painfully embarrassing or frustrating, depending on the circumstances.

If modern-day religious leaders were really interested in the welfare of their flocks, they would make sexual expression part of religious observances. In any event, both churches and individuals should become more active as go-betweens in the meeting and mating ritual.

Hot Tubs

One of the primary tenets of Shintoism, the native religion of Japan, is cleanliness. Because of it, the Japanese very early in their history developed the custom of taking daily hot baths. Since nudity in itself was not considered sinful, sexual, or licentious, the Japanese did not distinguish between the sexes when bathing. Also, because the conservation of water and heating materials was part of their upbringing, the Japanese developed the system of scrubbing themselves clean before entering the bath to soak, so several people could enjoy the benefits of the same tub of hot water.

Christianity, on the other hand, did not associate cleanliness with godliness. Instead, bathing was associated with sex and sin, and for much of the history of Europe it was, if not actually forbidden, certainly not encouraged by the church. When the first Westerners arrived in Japan, they were shocked to learn that the Japanese bathed every day. They were even more shocked when they discovered that the Japanese sexes bathed together. Portuguese and Spanish missionaries who arrived in Japan in the mid 1500s allowed their converts to bathe only every other week.

Three hundred years later, when American missionaries began flocking to Japan, their converts were allowed to bathe once a week, but mixed bathing was an absolute no-no.

The Japanese were just as shocked at the Westerners—first, because they bathed so infrequently and reeked with offensive odors and, second, because they regarded mixed bathing as a sin in the eyes of their god.

I converted to mixed-sex bathing very early in my years in Japan—within the first week, I believe. I have since been a strong advocate of the practice.

Perhaps the single most important benefit from mixed-sex bathing is that it helps prevent hangups about the human body in general and the various sex organs in particular. Thus, in just one activity, a substantial amount of the stress, the suffering, and the ruined lives that result from sex-related problems could be eliminated from American society if we adopted the practice of mixed bathing from childhood on.

There are other benefits to deep, hot-tub soaking, regardless of whether one does it with members of the opposite sex. It is physically and mentally relaxing and rejuvenates the spirit. There is nothing quite like it after a tiring day. Of course, it is far more pleasant and rewarding when done with family members and friends—when it is a deeply satisfying social, as well as spiritual, experience.

Fortunately, there is already a growing tendency toward hot-tub togetherness in the country. The challenge is to sell it to enough people that the prevailing social institutions will sanction it and allow it to find its own natural pace of development. But just mixed bathing at home is not enough for our society at large to get the help it needs. For the full benefit, we would have to license and build public bathhouses where anyone could go for a modest fee, just as the Japanese have done for centuries—reversing, of course, the present law in Japan that requires separate bathing areas for men and women. This law was passed in the 1950s as the result of agitation by a few Westernized women in the Diet who accepted the American premise that the practice was demeaning to women.

Mixed bathing does not in itself demean or mock anybody. These are emotional reactions of people who have developed sexual hangups as a result of the irrational behavior we would like to see eliminated. For most of us, mixed bathing is both a humbling and humanizing experience. Even those who are so beautifully endowed physically that they can't help but show off eventually learn that time changes everything and that they become just one of the crowd.

It is difficult for people to be arrogant, pompous, or falsely pious when they are stark naked. Let us all work toward the day when we have nothing to hide from each other.

EDUCATION

When American military and civilian Occupation personnel began restructuring Japan's educational system soon after the beginning of the postwar Occupation in 1945, one of the first things they went after was the Japanese emphasis on *shushin*, or "moral education." It was eliminated from their educational system.

The American belief was that *shushin*, which emphasized fealty to the Emperor, nationalism, filial piety, and loyalty, was responsible for the militaristic and warlike characteristic of the Japanese. In their well-intentioned attempt to make the Japanese less militaristic, the Americans threw out the good with the bad, leaving the Japanese educational system with no program for teaching morality, which in its simplest context is respect for the common good.

Japanese educators and government bureaucrats, as well, had mixed feelings about the elimination of *shushin* from the national curriculum. The overwhelming majority of them were not in favor of a return to the ultranationalistic education of the past, but they realized that without a solid basis in morality, the young people of Japan would be unsuitable for society. In 1957, five years after they regained sovereignty, the Japanese reinstated the teaching of morality in their schools. But this time it was called *dotoku*, or "morality," and was based on the Confucian concept that success in life is determined by academic achievement and respect for the rights of others.

Young Japanese take great pride in being students. During their school years, they develop a strong sense of identity, self-worth, and obligation to their families and their schools, which is later carried on to their companies and the country. The result is that the Japanese not only have a national identity and national ethic, they also have similar national goals.

We in the United States are just coming around to realizing that we, too, need to absorb a moral foundation for our thoughts and actions when we are young—a need that is not now and never has been adequately fulfilled by religions or parents. We appear to be afraid of moral education because of the religious connotation that we automatically give it.

Because our young people are not taught to believe in and abide by a rational, coherent ethical system, unethical behavior has virtually become the norm in many professions and areas of life. Doctors and hospitals exploit patients and the government. The misrepresentation and misuse of drugs is rampant in the pharmaceutical and medical industries. A retired owner of a construction company says, "There is cheating on every level of the building industry in the U.S." The unethical practices of lawyers adds hundreds of millions of dollars a year to the cost of doing business.

We would be well served at this time to adopt the Confucian philosophy as it has been modernized by the Japanese. Being a philosophy and not a religion, it would not be an immediate threat to any religion; and, being close enough to the old, idealistic American ethic of honesty, hard work, and sacrifice, it might also get by Congress, scholars, and educators.

Japanese children attend school 240 days out of the year, compared to 178 days a year for American students. Japanese students study several hours a week more than the average American students. Japanese students consistently score higher than American students in math and science tests. In recent surveys, the average score of the highest-achieving American students was below the worst-performing Japanese students. There is speculation that one of the reasons why the Japanese are better at math than Americans is because of their use of the abacus, which teaches math concepts and mental skills in mathematical reasoning.

Until they enter a university, Japanese students study more and harder than American students for many reasons, but in general terms because the system of education, including family support and discipline, is far better organized, better administered, and more efficient.

The key figure in the education of the Japanese is the Japanese mother. In brief, the primary function of most Japanese mothers is to see that their children get the best possible education. They devote a major portion of their time, energy, and emotions to supporting their children's educational efforts by creating and maintaining a nurturing system that conditions the children to try their very best.

The most conscientious of these mothers are known in Japanese as *kyoiku-mama*, or "education mothers," meaning that the education of their children is virtually their whole life.

The approach taken by Japanese mothers is quite different from the methods used by American parents in their attempts to encourage their children to study and do well in school. American parents get angry, loud, and punitive, which results in the erection of a barrier between them and their children. In many cases, American children give up trying just to spite their parents and to express personal independence from parental tyranny.

Japanese mothers, on the other hand, develop a deeper and more consistent personal and emotional relationship with their children. They constantly remind their children of the sacrifice they are making on their behalf and emphasize that the children are the most important thing in the world to them.

Instead of showing anger and frustration and punishing their children when they slack off in their efforts to learn, Japanese mothers quietly and calmly—but relentlessly—tell the children that they are disappointed and hurt.

The love-and-dependence relationship between Japanese mothers and their children is so deep and so strong that this kind of emotional appeal usually motivates the children to apply themselves heroically to the task at hand. Some Japanese mothers put their children under intense personal obligation to do their utmost and are extremely careful to make sure the relationship between them and their children is so harmonious and supportive that the children willingly do their best.

The bond that is developed between Japanese mothers and their children is described as *amae*, which encompasses love, dependency, emotional satisfaction, and more. It is a kind of love that is held together by a strong sense of mutual dependence and obligation. *Amae*, as we learned earlier, is the foundation for all personal relationships in Japanese society, including, to a considerable extent, business.

I am not suggesting that American mothers become instant *kyoiku-mama*. That would be impossible, of course, but I do recommend that American parents stop trying to force their children to study through threats and punishment and make their appeals emotional in a very quiet and supportive manner. In other words, "If you love me, if you appreciate what I am doing for you, please show me by studying hard."

The Abacus

In this day of computers and other electronic wizardry, it might seem idiotic to suggest that the *soroban*, the ancient abacus from China, be introduced into the American school system. But, as the Japanese have discovered, the abacus is far more than a mathematical Ouija board.

The Japanese imported the *soroban* from China in the 1500s, and it very quickly became a vital part of their everyday life, influencing not only the conduct of business, but the manual and mental dexterity of the people.

The use of the *soroban* in Japan waned rapidly with the introduction of small, pocket electronic calculators in the 1950s and 60s, but it has made a comeback in recent years and is now preferred by many businesses over computers. Banks and other financial institutions in particular have found that *soroban* users are less apt to make mistakes than computer operators and that using the *soroban* is less tiring and less boring than using a computer.

The main point is that the *soroban* requires both physical and mental skill to use properly and quickly, and this challenge is part of its attraction. Some people in the United States are already using the *soroban*. In fact, there is a Soroban Institute at the University of Southern California, founded by Dr. Leo Richards. Richards maintains that the *soroban* is of extraordinary value in the psychological process of learning. He says it instills discipline and confidence and that it makes the learning of mathematics a hands-on experience that is fun.

Japan's National Abacus Education Federation says that the *soroban* removes a lot of the intimidating mystery from math and can turn a mathematical duffer into a whiz kid. Those who believe the *soroban* is too slow and too inexact to compete with computers are in for a surprise. In a number of contests between *soroban* and computers in Tokyo and London, the *soroban* users not only held their own, they also won a number of the contests.

This is one simple, mechanical artifact we can import from Japan—or manufacture here—that could result in a significant improvement in the mental and physical development of our youth, as well as have a positive effect on their behavior in school.

Body/Mind Training

Two of Japan's most popular martial arts, judo and karate, have already made significant advances in the U.S. There are hundreds of judo and karate schools around the country with thousands of students. I would like to see both of these arts institutionalized in the American educational system, beginning with the first year of elementary school.

Judo and karate are not just physical skills that make it possible for the adept person to crack a stack of bricks or flip someone head over heels. They include strict training in both physical and mental discipline, as well as spiritual values. Students of karate and judo are taught sportsmanship, respect for the rights of others, and the meaning and importance of loyalty and honor. The combination of physical skills, discipline, ethics, and morality that make up the way of judo and karate are just the kind of thing most American children do not get from their parents or the present school system.

Of course, being even fairly skilled at one or the other of these two arts does wonders for one's self-confidence and ego. In addition, bullies of all ages would be less apt to pick on people who know how to defend themselves, and that knowledge would be a deterrent to muggings and physical assaults. Parity in power works just as well for individuals as it does for nations.

Another Japanese martial art that should be widely practiced in the U.S. is *kendo*, or "The Way of the Sword" (sword-fighting). The Samurai of Japan's feudal age (1192–1868) were, as a group, the greatest swordsmen the world has ever seen. The more famous masters of this then-deadly serious art practiced for several hours a day for 30 or more years, until they were so skillful they could successfully engage several opponents at the same time in battles to the death.

This tradition has been carried on by kendo enthusiasts in Japan today, but real swords and the rigid wooden staves once used in training and exhibition bouts have been replaced by a less deadly weapon made of flexible bamboo. Opponents wear helmets, face masks, and padded garments on their upper torso, much like football players.

Kendo is a form of one-on-one combat that requires a combination of a sharp mind, fast reflexes, speed, agility, intense concentration, and courage. While judo and karate practitioners can demonstrate their ability in various forms of solo exhibitions, the kendoist must contest a live opponent to demonstrate mastery of form and ability. Kendo is therefore a more demanding art and is highly prized by the Japanese for its character-building value—something we could use more of in the U.S.

It is probably too intense, too physical to be accepted in American schools, but I believe it could become as much of a commercial success as judo and karate have been, and I would like to see *kendo* gyms in every community.

In the sixth and seventh centuries in Japan, the priesthood and aristocracy began using China's ancient ideograms, called *kanji* in Japanese, to write their own language, while retaining both the structure and pronunciation of their native tongue. A few generations later, Japanese scholars developed two sets of phonetic syllables to express the parts of Japanese that could not be rendered in Chinese characters. These two syllabaries were called *hiragana* and *katakana*.

Kanji, along with these phonetic signs, gradually became the way all educated Japanese wrote their language. Since there are nearly 50,000 *kanji* in all, memorizing and learning how to draw even one-tenth of them was a lifelong challenge.

Over the centuries, the time and energy required to learn how to write—actually to draw—the thousands of characters and the skills developed as a result of the effort were a primary force in the development of the manual dexterity, artistry, and even the character and personality of the Japanese. In fact, for a long period in Japan's history, skill in drawing the characters was equated with the ethics and morality of the individual.

The *amae* (selfless dependence) factor in all interpersonal relationships, the social principles of *giri* (obligations) and *ninjo* (human feelings), the importance of *shibumi* (refined simplicity), and their aesthetics—all these are vital aspects of the Japanese character, but there is something else, something that I and many others have referred to and danced around but not really pinpointed.

I am greatly indebted to my friend and colleague Dan Nakatsu of San Francisco, who spent many years in Japan as an advertising executive, consultant, inventor, and speechwriter for Japanese executives, for finally focusing my attention on this mainspring of Japanese character by first of all labeling it and then expounding on its demonstrable influence.

Dan first pointed out that there had to be something beyond the aesthetics, the stylized manners, the animistic philosophy, the insularism, and even the ambitions of the Japanese to explain their obsession with order, precision, group-think, consensus and cooperation—the characteristics that have contributed so much to their rapid rise to prominence in the world economic order. This "something" was their writing system.

The primary commonality that all Japanese share, the main source and force of their Japaneseness, is their language and the process of learning how to speak it and write it. It is this writing process, the *kaki-kata*, or way of writing, that is one of the principal keys of the formation of the Japanese character.

From the beginning, there was only one way to draw each of the *kanji*, and each Japanese student was meticulously drilled in this one way, over and over. The process was not only mechanical. It was aesthetic and metaphysical. The *kanji* were pictures of things, of ideas—not just symbols of sounds, as in the English alphabet.

This concentrated conditioning in the *kaki-kata* of *kanji* molds the physical abilities, as well as the mental cast of the Japanese. It develops dexterity and skill with the hands. It develops a sense of propriety, precision, style, and beauty. It develops a spirit of cohesion, cooperation, and national identity. It conditions the Japanese for regimentation. It disciplines their thought processes. It homogenizes them.

Learning how to write the complicated ideograms is still a major undertaking in the educational process of every Japanese. Until shortly after the end of World War II, all Japanese were expected to learn how to read and write at least 3,000 of the figures. Some scholarly works required a knowledge of 5,000–6,000 *kanji*. After the end of World War II, the Education Ministry of Japan decreed that only 1,854 of the characters would be required in the public school system and that newspapers, magazines, and other such publications should be limited to this number of characters to simplify the educational process.

Still today, the effort required to master 1,854 *kanji* is formidable and plays a key role in the formation of the Japanese. Becoming skilled in drawing the characters is an education in itself. The rendering of the Chinese ideograms has never been approached as a static, mechanical skill. It has traditionally been considered an art, and those who became especially good at it won fame as artists.

This training, which Japanese children begin as soon as they enter any kind of school, helps mold their character and their knowledge of the culture, shapes their image of themselves, sharpens their ability to concentrate and remember, hones their aesthetic ability, develops a fine sense of balance and harmony, builds patience and perseverance, and makes each one of them an artist of no little skill.

The learning and writing of *kanji* is one of the most powerful forces in the making of a Japanese. If the Japanese cherish their essence, their uniqueness, the characteristics that give them an edge over many other people, they will not scrap or further diminish the *kanji* system of writing their language, as some nearsighted individuals now advocate.

The introduction in the mid-1980s of word processors that can write Japanese will probably make this point moot, however. There is surely no way the Japanese can maintain their system of writing in the face of the revolution now going on in communications around the world. The effect this will have on future generations of Japanese will be profound.

While it is tempting to suggest that the art of *kanji* be introduced into the American educational system, because we could use all of the benefit of the discipline and character traits it develops, there would be far too many barriers and objections.

What we could do, however, is reintroduce the practice of penmanship and calligraphy in American schools, making both of them required courses and requiring a high standard of proficiency before anyone was allowed to graduate from elementary school.

A Japanese Miscellany

Business Cards

One example of a Japanese custom that is gradually being adopted in the U.S. (and which I have been advocating for decades) is for regular employees of companies to have business cards, featuring the company logo, their department and title, or some variation. Reese Haggott, executive vice president of Alpine Electronics of America Inc., says that issuing business cards to all of his company's employees resulted in a profound boost in their morale and a sense of pride in themselves and the company.

A businessman in Japan without a name card is virtually a nonperson because ceremonial exchange of cards is a vital part of personal and professional relationships in a vertically structured society. We do not need to go that far, but we can improve on the use of name cards by doing something typically American—putting our photographs and other business or personal information on the cards; something few Japanese would dare to do. I have been doing this since the 1950s, with very positive results in both the U.S. and Japan, and I now see a number of specialized companies around the U.S. offering full-color cards that are very attractive company advertisements. One of the more successful of these companies, founded by young entrepreneur Ed Zito, is Positive Concepts Ltd., in Lithia Springs, Georgia.

Handicrafts

Throughout its history, Japan has been divided into regions, fiefs, or provinces, first by geography and climate, then for political reasons. Until recent times, each of these districts was isolated enough that it had to be more or less self-sufficient. Many of the products developed in the different provinces or regions were unique or distinctive and became popular among Japanese travelers as souvenirs and gift items. Gradually the fame of the products spread throughout the country, and they came to be known as *Meibutsu*, or "Famous Products." It became almost obligatory that travelers buy one or more of these *meibutsu* in every district they visited. Thus the production of these items developed into important local handicraft industries.

Today Japan's *meibutsu* continue to play a major role in local economies, as well as in exports, since virtually every foreign visitor to Japan also buys several *meibutsu* as personal souvenirs or gifts for families and friends. The *meibutsu* industry is well organized on both a local and national level. The products are available in numerous convenient retail outlets, particularly those that cater to travelers. And, just as important, they are identified as *meibutsu* not only in their labeling, but also in advertising.

The United States is several generations behind Japan in the development, promotion, and merchandising of its local handicrafts, of its own *meibutsu*. The one complaint that is heard over and over from foreign visitors to the United States is, "Where can I find things to buy that are made-in-America?" Surveys made by the U.S. Travel Service reveal that local economies around the country would be enriched by millions of dollars of additional income a year if their *meibutsu* industries were better organized and their products better merchandised.

There are thousands of *meibutsu* in America that are known only to local residents who are involved in the industries and to the tourists who happen onto them during visits. Some of these products have histories that go back to Colonial days and are a part of the cultural heritage of the country.

I suggest that we copy the Japanese system in promoting and marketing our *meibutsu* and that the tourism development offices of all the states be charged with the responsibility of identifying all of the *meibutsu* industries in their areas, preparing directories of the makers and their products, and making these directories available to the local travel and retail industries. Sales of such products could be increased dramatically not only to foreign visitors, but to American travelers, as well.

Haircuts

Japanese barbers have converted many foreigners to rabid Japanophilia. The Japanese are not inherently better barbers, but they are more painstaking and meticulous about the operation, and it certainly feels as if you are getting a better haircut or shave or whatever.

What really distinguishes Japanese barbers, however, is that they pamper the customer, first by taking time to be careful and conscientious, and then by giving each customer a relaxing head and shoulder massage before the final cleanup.

This attention to detail, plus the personal physical care, is in keeping with age-old Japanese traditions that developed when time was measured in seasons instead of minutes, hours, or even days, and is part of the hedonism of Japan's unique culture.

Getting a haircut in Japan is a sensual experience, and it is equivalent to the grooming that characterizes lower primates. It helps satisfy the need we all have for being touched and caressed and serves a deeper, more fundamental purpose than just a desire to be well groomed.

I therefore highly recommend that American barbershops emulate this popular Japanese tradition. It would significantly change the atmosphere of the typical barbershop, encouraging men to visit their barbers more often and improve their overall appearance.

Taxis

By most standards, Japan has the best taxicab system, the best taxi drivers, and the best taxis in the world. If we did nothing else but emulate this extraordinary example of their character, personality, and achievements, the U.S. would be far ahead.

Granted, there are far more people in Japan who use taxis than in the U.S. and it is therefore a far more profitable industry that can afford a standard of service not approached in this country. The point is, however, that the service must improve before the industry can make significant advances.

Once again, we go back to human character and motivation. Most Japanese taxis are kept scrupulously clean. Their drivers take personal responsibility for keeping their cabs immaculate. Owner-drivers are even more zealous in the care and cleanliness of their cars. Many of them have installed white seat covers. Many have tiny portable TV sets for the convenience of their passengers. Some even keep fresh flowers in their cabs.

The typical Japanese taxi driver is honest, sincere, and trustworthy. A taxi driver deliberately taking a roundabout route to boost the fare is rare. Most Japanese taxi drivers treat passengers as valued customers and are polite to them, including those who are drunk and unruly. Japanese taxi drivers keep themselves neat and clean. They do not look like bums or street derelicts, which seems to be the look preferred by a significant percentage of their American counterparts.

Japanese taxis are outfitted with doors (on the sidewalk side) that the driver opens and closes with the flick of a switch. The automatic doors are especially convenient when you have packages or luggage in your hands, and they are another factor in the Japanese way of providing as much service and convenience as possible instead of doing just enough to get by.

One Japanese taxi company in Kyoto advertises that any passenger can refuse to pay the fare if its drivers neglect to express their gratitude for the business or to thank the passenger. The drivers in this company are required to attend lectures on various business subjects, including high-technology in order to converse intelligently with businessmen passengers and to *act as information referral services* on behalf of their clientele. Of course, this company is an exception. But it is a lesson in the thinking and ambitions of the Japanese.

Law and Order

Virtually every American who has been to Japan has been impressed with the street-corner *koban* ("police boxes") they see all over the country in cities and towns, as well as rural areas. Many of these Americans have wondered out loud why we can't adopt the same approach to security and law enforcement.

The *koban* system began in Edo (Tokyo) in 1628, when the Tokugawa Shogunate finally heeded the pleas of townspeople to provide them with protection from rowdy and oftentimes murderous Samurai warriors, who no longer had any wars to fight and whose code of Bushido ethics had weakened. Street-killings by rogue Samurai were so common they were known as *Tsuji-Giri*, or "Street-Corner Killings."

The first street-corner police-posts were under the jurisdiction of the city magistrate (*bugyo*) and were known as *Suji Ban*, or "Corner Guards." The idea was popular with the common people, and soon thereafter the various *Daimyo* (Feudal Lords), who were required to maintain residences and their families in Edo, along with high-ranking Shogunate retainers, also established their own systems of *koban*. At one time during the Tokugawa period, there were 898 *koban* in Edo alone.

When the Tokugawa Shogunate fell in 1868 and modern police methods were introduced into Japan, the *koban* system was continued. When the American Occupation forces took over Japan in 1945, they closed most of the *koban* and instituted the American system of patrolling by vehicle.

As soon as the Occupation ended, the Japanese went back to the familiar and effective *koban*. Besides watching over their neighborhoods and being on call when needed, the police who man the *koban* act as information sources for their areas, especially helping people locate addresses (because most streets in Japan do not have names, and addresses of homes or buildings have nothing to do with the street they may be on or near).

Another of the more interesting services provided by the police manning the street-corner stations is lending taxi fares to revelers who miss the last trains or subways and have spent all their money.

There are two types and two sizes of *koban* in Japan. The larger ones are located in business/shopping sections of cities and are manned by several policemen. The smaller ones, in residential areas, have one or two officers on duty at all times.

Like the casual American visitors who are immediately attracted to the *koban* system, I believe it should be adopted in the United States. It gives the police a solid presence in every section of a town or city. It puts them within walking or running distance of many of the places of business and the people they are charged with protecting.

The presence of policemen permanently stationed in *koban* scattered around the cities would have a dampening effect on the audacity of bank robbers, burglars, muggers, and other criminal types who now prey on residents and businesses alike— with a better than even chance of not getting caught.

At present, Tokyo has 1,244 *koban*, with a staff of over 15,000 police officers—or one-third of the city's total police force. Besides patrolling their neighborhoods, answering questions, helping drunks make it home, settling domestic squabbles, and acting as lost-and-found drop-off points, they also keep an eye on elderly people living alone in their districts—all services that would be welcomed by the American public.

Belly Wrappers

Observant visitors who spend any length of time in Japan may notice that older Japanese men and some members of the laboring class, particularly those who work outside in all kinds of weather, often wear a thick wool band around their abdomens. This band is called a *haramaki*, or "belly wrapper," and its use is a traditional custom that grew out of the belief that the center of one's being is located in the abdomen and that it should be kept warm.

The *haramaki* custom is gradually diminishing in Japan as traditions weaken and the old-timers die off, but it has enough merit, I believe, that it should be preserved by the Japanese and adopted in the United States, as well.

The belief that the seat of life is below the belt rather than above it has been common enough in world cultures to make one suspect that there might be something to it. We know only too well that the heart has nothing to do with ruling the spirit, and there is some doubt about the brain.

One of my own metaphysical experiences would seem to give the abdomen more prominence than it usually gets in the West. I was alone in a Japanese-style room in the Yoyogi-Uehera section of Tokyo in the mid-1950s. It was a rainy afternoon, fraught with an atmosphere of intimate relationship between myself and my surroundings.

I had been studying Japanese history for several hours, and I was tired. I stopped, relaxed totally, and turned my mind loose. All at once, in the space of about three seconds, my consciousness left my head and floated down to my abdomen. It was a completely unexpected and fascinating experience. I was surprised—almost stunned—by the phenomenon. I felt a pleasant, sensual glow spreading throughout my body, as if I were going to have a spiritual climax.

"My God!" I thought. "This is fantastic!"

And I began to push and strain in order to speed up the spreading of the glow and make it stronger. But as soon as I made an effort to control the process, my mind literally flashed back to its usual resting place. I was disappointed and tried for several minutes to float my mind free again. I came close for a few brief seconds, but then it rebounded into my cranium and, as far as my waking hours are concerned, it has apparently remained there ever since.

Countless other stories about visceral awareness have been recorded (by more reputable reporters than I), making it fairly certain that the abdomen is indeed something more than just a digestive factory. I therefore recommend that Americans, especially older men whose blood has begun to cool down, adopt the *haramaki* custom. There is no evidence that it does any harm, and the reward could be a longer and more useful life. It would certainly be an interesting conversational piece, especially in some circumstances that I can imagine.

About the Author

Boye De Mente first went to Japan in 1949 as a member of the Army Security Agency, assigned to an intelligence processing unit in Tokyo. Since then, his involvement with Japan has been intimate and ongoing, having worked for the Japan Travel Bureau and been editor of several major publications in Japan, including *Preview* magazine, the *Far East Reporter*, *Today's Japan*, and *The Importer*. De Mente has written more than a dozen books on Japan, its culture, and language. Today, in addition to writing and consulting on Japan, De Mente is senior editor of *Far East Traveler* magazine in Tokyo and executive editor of *Japan Journal*, with editorial offices in Tokyo and Marina Del Rey, California. De Mente makes his home in Paradise Valley, Arizona. He is married with two daughters.

LANGUAGE AND TRAVEL BOOKS
FROM PASSPORT BOOKS

Dictionaries and References
Vox Spanish and English Dictionaries
Harrap's Concise Spanish and English
  Dictionary
Harrap's French and English Dictionaries
Klett German and English Dictionary
Harrap's Concise German and English
  Dictionary
Everyday American English Dictionary
Beginner's Dictionary of American
  English Usage
Diccionario Inglés
El Diccionario del Español Chicano
Diccionario Básico Norteamericano
British/American Language Dictionary
The French Businessmate
The German Businessmate
The Spanish Businessmate
Harrap's Slang Dictionary (French and English)
English Picture Dictionary
French Picture Dictionary
Spanish Picture Dictionary
German Picture Dictionary
Guide to Spanish Idioms
Guide to German Idioms
Guide to French Idioms
Guide to Correspondence in Spanish
Guide to Correspondence in French
Español para los Hispanos
Business Russian
Yes! You Can Learn a Foreign Language
Everyday Japanese
Japanese in Plain English
Korean in Plain English
Robin Hyman's Dictionary of Quotations
NTC's American Idioms Dictionary
Passport's Japan Almanac
Japanese Etiquette and Ethics in
  Business
How To Do Business With The Japanese
Korean Etiquette And Ethics In Business

Verb References
Complete Handbook of Spanish Verbs
Spanish Verb Drills
French Verb Drills
German Verb Drills

Grammar References
Spanish Verbs and Essentials of Grammar
Nice 'n Easy Spanish Grammar
French Verbs and Essentials of Grammar
Nice 'n Easy French Grammar
German Verbs and Essentials of Grammar
Nice 'n Easy German Grammar
Italian Verbs and Essentials of Grammar
Essentials of Russian Grammar

Welcome Books
Welcome to Spain
Welcome to France
Welcome to Ancient Greece
Welcome to Ancient Rome

Language Programs
Just Listen 'n Learn: Spanish, French, Italian,
  German and Greek
Just Listen 'n Learn Plus: Spanish, French,
  and German
Practice & Improve Your . . . Spanish, French
  and German
Practice & Improve Your . . . Spanish, French and
  German PLUS
Japanese For Children
Basic French Conversation
Basic Spanish Conversation

Phrase Books
Just Enough Dutch
Just Enough French
Just Enough German
Just Enough Greek
Just Enough Italian
Just Enough Japanese
Just Enough Portuguese
Just Enough Scandinavian
Just Enough Serbo-Croat
Just Enough Spanish
Multilingual Phrase Book
International Traveler's Phrasebook

Language Game Books
Easy French Crossword Puzzles
Easy French Word Games and Puzzles
Easy Spanish Crossword Puzzles
Easy Spanish Word Games and Puzzles
Let's Learn About Series: Italy, France,
  Germany, Spain, America
Let's Learn Coloring Books In Spanish,
  French, German, Italian, And English

Humor in Five Languages
The Insult Dictionary: How to Give 'Em
  Hell in 5 Nasty Languages
The Lover's Dictionary: How to Be
  Amorous in 5 Delectable Languages

Technical Dictionaries
Complete Multilingual Dictionary of
  Computer Terminology
Complete Multilingual Dictionary of
  Aviation and Aeronautical Terminology
Complete Multilingual Dictionary of
  Advertising, Marketing and Communications
Harrap's French and English
  Business Dictionary
Harrap's French and English
  Science Dictionary

Travel
Nagel's Encyclopedia Guides
World at Its Best Travel Series
Runaway Travel Guides
Mystery Reader's Walking Guide: London
Japan Today
Japan at Night
Discovering Cultural Japan
Bon Voyage!
Business Capitals of the World
Hiking and Walking Guide to Europe
Frequent Flyer's Award Book
Ethnic London
European Atlas
Health Guide for International Travelers
Passport's Travel Paks: Britain, Italy,
  France, Germany, Spain
Passport's China Guides
On Your Own Series: Brazil, Israel
Spain Under the Sun Series: Barcelona, Toledo,
  Seville and Marbella

Getting Started Books
Introductory language books for Spanish,
  French, German and Italian.

For Beginners Series
Introductory language books for children
  in Spanish, French, German and Italian.

PASSPORT BOOKS

a division of NTC *Publishing Group*
4255 West Touhy Avenue
Lincolnwood, Illinois 60646-1975